Ministry

Ministry

A case for change

Edward Schillebeeckx

SCM PRESS LTD

Translated by John Bowden from the Dutch
Kerkelijk ambt,
published by Uitgeverij H. Nelissen BV,
Bloemendaal, Holland, 1980

334 02171 5

First published in English 1981
by SCM Press Ltd.
58 Bloomsbury Street, London WC1
Second impression 1982

Photoset by Input Typesetting Ltd.
and printed in Great Britain by
Billing and Sons Ltd.
London & Worcester

Foreword

I have written about ministry on a number of occasions. I have done so directly, above all in 'Priesterschap en episcopaat', *Tijdschrift voor Geestelijk Leven* 11, 1955, 52–63; 'Handoplegging', in *Theologisch Woordenboek*, Vol. 2, Roermond 1957, cols. 2143–6; 'Priesterschap', op. cit., Vol. 3, Roermond 1958, cols. 3959–4003; 'Merkteken', op. cit., Vol. 2., cols. 3231–7; 'Wijding', op. cit., Vol. 3, cols. 4967–82; 'Het apostolisch ambt van de kerkelijke hiërarchie', *Studia Catholica* 32, 1957, 258–90; 'Dogmatiek van ambt en lekestaat', *Tijdschrift voor Theologie* 2, 1962, 258–94; 'Bezinning en apostolaat in het leven der seculiere en reguliere priesters', in *Tijdschrift voor Geestelijk Leven* 19, 1963, 307–29; 'Communicatie tussen priesters en leek', *Nederlandse Katholieke Stemmen* 59, 1963, 210–22; 'Het celibaat van de priester', in *Tijdschrift voor Theologie* 5, 1965, 296–329; 'Het ambtscelibaat in de branding', Bilthoven 1966; 'Theologische kanttekeningen bij de huidige priestercrisis', *Tijdschrift voor Theologie* 8, 1968, 402–34; 'De priester op de synode van 1971', in *Aan mensen gewaagd. Zicht op de identiteit van de priester*, Tielt-Utrecht 1972, 241–86; 'The Problem of the Infallibility of the Church's Office – A Theological Reflection', *Concilium* 9, 1973, no. 3, 77–94; 'Basis en Ambt. Ambt in dienst van nieuwe gemeentevorming', in *Basis en Ambt*, Bloemendaal 1979, 43–90; 'Creatieve terugblik als inspiratie voor het ambt in de toekomst', *Tijdschrift voor Theologie* 19, 1979, 266–93 (English translation in *Minister? Pastor? Prophet?*, SCM Press and Crossroad Publishing Co 1980); 'The Christian Community and its Office-Bearers', *Concilium* 133, 1980, 95–133.

These publications cover a period of about twenty-five years and have also gradually come to be a reflection of the growing 'crisis over the priesthood'. It was not my purpose to work up all this material into what then, as in former times, would have to have been called 'a complete theology of the ministry'. Four articles (those in *Aan mensen gewaagd*, 1972; in *Basis en Ambt*,

1979; in *Tijdschrift voor Theologie*, 1979; and in *Concilium*, 1980), formed the starting point of this book. I have worked over these four articles and expanded them, added a number of other chapters, revised some points of detail and strengthened their basic thesis in many places with new historical data and more rigorous argument. Finally, all the material has been welded into a new unity.

A theologian knows that what he says will not be welcome to everyone. However, convinced as he is of the liberating power of the truth (including the historical truth) which he is honour bound to pursue, he does not have the right to impose censorship in advance on his own insights: he is obliged to make public the results of his investigation.

Historical arguments can be countered only by historical arguments to the contrary.

Nijmegen, 10 August 1980, the anniversary of my ordination to the priesthood

Contents

Introduction

'No Church Community without One or More Leaders'

'*Ecclesia non est quae non habet sacerdotes*,' wrote the church father Jerome: 'There can be no church community without a leader or team of leaders.'[1] In saying this he was, of course, expressing the general view of the early church. This patristic comment is a judgment in advance on the way in which many of us today take the shortage of priests for granted. If, sociologically speaking, there seems to be such a shortage of priests, something has gone wrong with the way in which believers look at their church and those who hold office in it (and with the way in which they put their views into practice).

However, it is impossible to restrict oneself to a purely sociological and statistical analysis of the present shortage of priests.[2] As a good deal of information and statistical surveys show, this gives rise to questionable side-effects in the church and above all in the eucharist, because of its dubious ideological background.[3] It is also important to make a historical, theological and ecclesiological diagnosis. Such a theological investigation begins to show up the historical obstructions and prejudices which can also be found at the origins of the present shortage of priests and which need not be there if we are aware of the theology of the church, i.e. of what makes up a Christian church community.

Much is possible in a church of Christ, but not everything. The fact that I am looking back (albeit in a quite wide-ranging way) on conceptions of the ministry in the first ten centuries in order to compare them with conceptions in the second Christian millennium is in no way the result of an untheological romanticism about Christian origins. Far less is it the result of what I would feel to be the false view that chronology, viz., closeness in time to the New Testament, should be given some preference as such. In themselves, the first ten centuries of Christianity do not have any priority over the second Christian millennium. What is decisive here is not chronology, but Christian practice, the following of Jesus. However, loyalty to the New Testament and to the great Christian tradition which has now lasted for almost two thousand years in no way means repetition of any particular period, even of the time of the New Testament. But without critical recollection of the whole of the church's past, our modern questions are not in themselves normative either, although they are part of the picture. Only in a mutually critical pastoral, practical and theological confrontation between the present and the past is a truly Christian answer possible.

I am therefore essentially concerned with theological criteria: with the theological significance of the church's practice of the ministry (albeit on each occasion in very precise historical settings). These criteria are provided by the living life of the communities which take initiatives; the theologian can do no more than reflect on them. The critical point – in every sense of the phrase – is whether the practice of the ministry (albeit on each occasion in a very precise historical setting) is shaped primarily by theological criteria, or on the basis of non-theological factors. Or more precisely, whether it is formed from theological reflection on new human and cultural situations.

One of the tasks of the theologians is to confront the church and its living practice on occasion with the whole of the tradition of faith, all its historically changing contexts, and the theological or non-theological models which are invested in them, whether consciously or unconsciously. For all its importance, even the Council of Trent is only one of the many regulating factors in the correct interpretation of scripture. Thus it in no way expresses the many-sided totality of Christian faith; it is only a segment of that, and is so in a very limited historical situation, which is exclusively that of the Western churches. Although this council, too, expressed 'Christian truth', it did so at all events in a particular context, i.e. in a specific way relating to a very definite Western situation. The consequence of this is that the statements of all councils, and particularly other, non-conciliar statements made by the church, must be interpreted not only within their own historical context but also with the whole of the Christian tradition of faith, as this gave orientation and inspiration to the further history of the church in the light of the biblical and apostolic faith. This is essential if we are to understand their significance for people now. For better or worse, then as now, this ongoing history of the church regularly gives renewed expression to inspiration in constantly new existential contexts. Here the Christian churches have sometimes done well, and sometimes less well, leading to disillusionment. We can regard all this as a generally accepted consensus among contemporary theologians, though the instruments of the church's teaching authority often have a tendency to dwell on 'the letter' of earlier statements and to underestimate their historical and hermeneutical dimensions.

If we are to be able to evaluate the possible theological significance of present-day new alternatives and forms of ministry which often deviate from the established order of the church, and are on the increase everywhere, we must steep ourselves in the facts of the history of the church: in antiquity, in the Middle Ages and in modern times. It will then also become clear that authoritative documents (the authority of which the Catholic theologian accepts, albeit not always to the same degree) are always prepared for by new practices which arise from the grass roots.

This applies both to those of the fifth century (the view of the priest held in the first millennium), those of the twelfth and thirteenth centuries (characteristic of the feudal view of the priest) and those of the sixteenth century (characteristic of the 'modern' Tridentine view of the priest and thus the view held by recent tradition). On each occasion official documents sanction a church practice which has grown up from the grass roots. At the present moment we can again see new alternatives or parallel views and practices, concerning the ministry in the church, developing from below. Of course these show a clear affinity to the biblical and patristic view of the ministry. So in the distant future we can expect the fulfilment of the expectation of an ultimate canonical sanctioning of what could be called the present-day, 'fourth phase' in the church's practice of the ministry (probably after a degree of purification). Critical remembrances of events in the past have a power to open up the future.

I

The Story of New Testament Communities

More than twenty years of biblical studies by commentators and theologians on ministry in the church, above all in the New Testament, have made a good deal clear, though in terms of exegesis a great many questions still remain unanswered.

1. The first Christian generation: the founders of the communities and those 'who labour among you, lead you and admonish you'

Apart from apostleship or the 'apostolate', the Christian communities did not receive any kind of church order from the hands of Jesus when he still shared our earthly history. Furthermore, 'the Twelve' were the symbol of the approaching eschatological community of God, which originally was not yet organized for a long-term earthly history. This primary, fundamental datum of the New Testament must already make us very cautious; we must not be led astray into speaking too casually about divine ordinances and particular dispositions in respect of the community and its leaders or ministry.

However, since according to the self-understanding of the first Christians the Christian community is a 'community of God',[1] a 'community of Christ',[2] and a 'temple of the Holy Spirit',[3] it is obvious that what developed spontaneously from below (as we would now put it, in accordance with the sociological laws of group formation) was recognized and explicitly interpreted by the communities, naturally and with good reason, indeed spontaneously, as a 'gift of the Lord' (Eph. 4.8–11; I Tim. 4.14; II Tim. 1.6). The New Testament, bubbling over with praise for 'blessings from above', does not know the later contrast between what comes 'from below' and what comes 'from above'. On the contrary, the whole community is the temple of the spirit, the body of Christ. Unless the whole community is unfaithful to the Lord in word or deed, what arises spontaneously from the community of Jesus is at the same time experienced as a gift of the Spirit. (Of course, this easy way of speaking also has a problematical reverse side, just as the later opposition between 'from above' and 'from below' also has a very problematical reverse side).

Within the New Testament, the texts compel us to make a distinction between two periods or phases which, though distinct, nevertheless flow into each other: the time of the 'apostles' and the post-apostolic period, though the latter is still within the New Testament. It is a fact that the first communities were founded by apostles. However, while the concept of 'apostleship' has a clearly defined nucleus, it is more fluid at the periphery. 'The Twelve' (later this becomes 'Peter with the Eleven') is a category which more than probably goes back to the earthly Jesus himself. It is a symbol of Israel's twelve patriarchs and tribes, and of the whole of Israel as a sign of the eschatological community of mankind. Luke above all (at a much later stage) worked out in his two books the concept of the 'apostolate' theologically in terms of the Twelve, in such a way that in fact he had some difficulty in recognizing Paul as an authentic apostle. Paul, at any rate, had not accompanied Jesus throughout the whole of his public ministry from his baptism in the Jordan until his death and the Easter experiences of the apostles afterwards (see Acts 1.21f.). However, in addition to this key concept of the Twelve, the primitive Christian concept of apostleship also includes many of the first Christians who had come forward before the founding of the first communities or before the building up of newly-founded communities. To begin with, there were also many enthusiasts here who in the earliest Christian period (and already in the old Q tradition) were called 'prophets'. Later, Eph. 2.20 speaks of 'apostles and prophets' as the foundation of the earliest Christian communities. Perhaps these prophets had not founded the communities themselves, but they were of great significance for their development. So in addition to the Twelve (about whose individual roles we know virtually nothing, apart from James and, to some extent, Peter), there were other 'apostles' who in fact presided over the birth of the first communities. At any rate, we should not forget that barely three years after Jesus' death (i.e. before Paul had become a Christian), intractable difficulties had arisen in Jerusalem, specifically between the Aramaic-speaking Christians – 'the Hebrews' (Acts 6.1) – and the Greek-speaking Jewish Christians there – 'the Hellenists', the so-called followers of Stephen. The occasion for these difficulties may have been some neglect on the part of the Aramaic-speaking Christians in providing material help to the Greek-speaking Jewish-Christian members of the community (Acts 6.15). However, all the signs are that the cause of this conflict lay deeper, because from the beginning the Greek-speaking Jews had other, wider expectations than the representatives of the accepted and somewhat rigid Jerusalem tradition, and they introduced these broader views into Christianity. The conflict was finally resolved when 'the apostles, together with all the community' (Acts 6.2) appointed seven members of the Greek-speaking Christian community in Jerusalem[4] to look after the Greek-speaking Jewish Christians in Jerusalem. Given Luke's interpretation (Acts 6.1–4), it is to some extent understandable that they were later called 'deacons', though this is historically incorrect; these so-called deacons, above all Philip 'the evangelist' (Acts 21.8), who was one of their number, did everything that the apostles did. In fact they were in a sense 'new apostles', although the Jerusalem community retained some oversight over their activity (Acts 8.14). Moreover, it was these Greek-speaking Jewish Christians who were persecuted by the Jewish Sanhedrin, while the Aramaic-speaking Christians were left undisturbed. Because of the persecutions they finally fled to Samaria and further north, to Syria. On the way these fugitives (especially under the leadership of Philip) founded many communities.[5] It is above all because of them that Christianity spread with such surprising speed throughout the whole of the ancient Near East. It was also from this group (remember Ananias in Antioch, Acts 22.12; 9.10–12; 9.17f.) that the later apostle Paul received his first initiation into the gospel of Jesus Christ. This Paul was to become the great bearer of the tradition and the pioneer of many Christian communities, above all of the communities about which we have the best historical information. By contrast, as is well known, not least because of conflicts within the early church, we have only scanty information about those communities which remained outside the influence of Paulinism (probably the so-called Matthaean and Johannine communities).

The Twelve, and the other apostles and prophets (cf. Acts 13.1–3), understood themselves to have been sent by their dead but risen Lord in the cause of Jesus, i.e. continuing the proclamation of the coming kingdom of God (see also Acts 20.25), and to be bound up with the action and the whole historical career and death of Jesus of Nazareth. The first communities received the faith from them on the basis of the personal experiences which most of them had had of Jesus, from his baptism in the Jordan until his death and their own Easter experiences afterwards.[6] Other founders of communities had obtained the content of their faith from what they had been told by older Christians, just as Paul had not known the earthly Jesus. On the basis of their origin and foundation, the Christian communities were therefore also characterized by apostolicity: they were apostolic churches. This essential characteristic was later to be taken up into the so-called apostolic creeds.[7] Of course, logically and also historically, apostolicity became an explicit theme only after the death of the apostles, in particular in the New Testament post-apostolic period, in which ecclesiology, the doctrine of the church and its ministry, was worked out more clearly. At any rate, when the apostles had died, the communities were more clearly conscious that they owed their Christian character to these founders. In other words, their foundation was apostolic and they therefore had to build further upon it. The second generation of Christians, who had come to know Jesus through the mediation of the 'apostles', began to call themselves apostolic in roughly the same way as, for example, the followers of Benedict began to call themselves Benedictines, i.e. not immediately, but at a later stage. For the New Testament, apostolicity is in the first instance a distinguishing title for the Christian community itself on the basis of the 'gospel of Jesus the Christ' which was proclaimed to it by the apostles, i.e. the gospel of reconciliation and the forgiveness of sins (see II Cor. 5.17–21; Matt. 18.15–18; John 20.21ff.).

In fact, for the most part these founders of communities were not local community leaders, but proclaimers of the gospel of Jesus, who were constantly on the move. However, Paul in particular sees a permanent *koinonia* or bond between founder and community (Gal. 6.6; Phil. 2.30; 4.14–17), which applies in both his own case and that of his fellow-workers. It was natural that when these missionary apostles moved on, their functions of leadership and co-ordination should be taken over by obvious and spontaneous leaders in the various communities (often the first converts and the first fellow workers, male or female, of the apostle); of course there is historical evidence for this. In the earliest writing of the New Testament, Paul already says to a community he has founded: 'We beseech you, brethren, to respect those who labour among you, lead you in the Lord and admonish you, and to esteem them very highly in love because of their work' (I Thess. 5.12; the three functions summarized are all governed by one article; see also Rom. 12.8f.). It is evident from this admonition of Paul's that within the communities, which understood themselves as brotherhoods, without rank or status, spontaneous leaders sometimes came up against the opposition of the brethren. Paul resolves the difficulty by pointing to the multiplicity of charismatic gifts given to members of the community, which include the gift of leading the community (in many different forms). Each has a particular task in the community. Although it is recognized as a particular charisma, the gift of leading the community still has no significance as a 'ministry' of the church; it is one of the many services which all the members of the community owe to each other, and each person cannot do everything. Thus originally the leaders of the community do not seem to have had any special name for their ministry ('those who labour among you, lead you and admonish you'). But the fact that there were local leaders in the communities even during the lifetime of the apostles, albeit ultimately under the oversight of the apostles, is historically undeniable. The leaders of the community also refer to these apostles when difficulties arise which they are uncertain how to resolve. Hence Paul's answer to a series of questions which had reached him from the community in Corinth (I Cor. 7.1).[8]

Local leaders of communities are not always the same as those whom Paul calls his 'fellow workers' (Rom. 16.3; I Thess. 3.2; II Cor. 8.23) 'in the work of the Lord' (I Cor. 15.58), fellow workers whom he evidently chose carefully and tested (see Phil. 2.19–24). They also seem to have included local community leaders, whom he mentions above all at the beginning of his letters (I Thess. 1.1; I Cor. 1.1; II Cor. 1.1; Philemon 1) or in the closing greetings (I Cor. 16.19f.; Rom. 16.3ff.; Phil. 4.21; Philemon 23f.). Paul calls all his fellow workers *sunergountes* (co-workers) and *kopiountes* (those who share concern and toil for the communities: I Thess. 5.12; I Cor. 16.16), '. . . who have devoted themselves to the service of the saints', i.e. the community: 'I urge you to be subject to such men and to every fellow worker and labourer' (I Cor. 16.16). Paul laid the foundation (I Cor, 3.10); they, the fellow workers, must continue to build upon it (*epoikodomein*), but they therefore also share in apostolic authority and privilege (above all I Cor. 9.6, 11f.; I Thess. 5.12–14; I Cor. 16.10–12) which Paul claims for himself on the basis of the Word of God (II Cor. 10.8; 13.10; I Thess. 2.13; 4.8). Over against the community, apostle and fellow workers are 'co-workers with God' (I Cor. 3.9.).

Paul gives pride of place among services within the community to prophesying and teaching (I Cor. 14.6; 12.28;

Rom. 12.6–8); so after the apostles he goes on to name 'prophets and teachers' as fellow workers of the apostles: 'And God has appointed in the church all kinds of people, first apostles, second prophets, third teachers' (I Cor. 12.28).[9] This mention occurs in the middle of a list of other services in the church: that of leading the community does not yet have the full significance of what ministry will later come to signify; at least, there was no reflection on this as long as the apostle was still alive. 'Prophets and teachers' were evidently general and technical terms in primitive Christianity for these incipient local leaders and pioneers in the Christian communities. We find them again not only later (when technical terms for the ministry had come into circulation), in Luke (Acts 13.1f.) and even in II Peter 3.2; 1.12–21, and moreover also in communities of a Matthaean type (Didache 15.1f.), but also in the intermediary period in the community at Ephesus ('apostles and prophets', Eph. 2.20, and 'pastors and teachers', Eph. 4.11).[10] Thus we can hardly claim that there were Pauline communities without leaders. Of course there were also house communities (I Cor. 16.19; Rom. 16.5; Philemon 2) alongside the larger local communities (I Cor. 14.23). Here the host and his wife played a leading role (thus Philemon and his wife Apphia, Philemon 1f.; 'Aquila and Prisca and the community at their house', I Cor. 16.19; 'Greet Prisca and Aquila, my fellow workers in Christ Jesus . . . and the community in their house', Rom. 16.3–5). The structuring of the community and its leadership follows the natural structure of a meeting of Christians in the home of a well-to-do fellow Christian; evidently, then, these too have fellow workers (see e.g. Archippus for the house community of Philemon and Apphia, Philemon 2).

As I have said, the names for the community leaders and those who work with the apostle are still in no way fixed. Paul speaks of 'those who labour for the community', of 'those who are over you', in the sense of members who have special responsibility for the community (I Thess. 5.12); in Philippi, general Greek terms are used: *episkopoi* in the sense of overseers, and their 'helpers' (deacons, but not in the technical sense). The names can differ, as is clear from a comparison between I Thess 5.12; I Cor. 12.28 and Phil. 1.1; and it is impossible to describe precisely what all these 'ministers' do for the sake of the ministry: they build on the foundation laid by Paul, each one according to his own gifts and talents. However, some are assigned a special place. In the Pauline communities, Timothy and Titus in particular are notable in this respect, even according to the authentic letters of Paul, and, moreover, at a very early stage (I Thess. 3.2; I Cor. 4.17; 16.10; II Cor. 7.6, 13, 14; Phil. 2.19ff.). Like Paul, these fellow workers of the apostle have authority over the community (I Thess. 5.12), and even over the local leaders of the community (e.g. over the overseers and helpers of Phil. 1.1, to whom Paul wants to send Timothy, Phil. 2.19–24). Paul's immediate fellow workers are evidently senior to local community leaders (II Cor. 8.16ff., 23).

Phil. 2.19–24 is of special importance in this respect. Philippians is an authentic letter of Paul (though there is dispute as to whether it is not a later combination of two authentic letters of Paul's). It is evident from this letter that Paul is reckoning that his life may be nearly at an end (Phil. 2.17). He therefore envisages sending Timothy to Philippi as 'his successor', responsible for care of the communities; he insists that in the last resort Timothy has the same authority as he does, as a faithful fellow worker, firm in the same faith. Although there is no 'legalism' here, Paul shows a certain concern over what will later be called 'apostolic succession'. The sending of Timothy (Phil. 2.19–24) is one which goes above the local leaders and shows all the marks of being a 'succession' to the apostle Paul. However, the basis of this succession is 'the community of faith' between Paul and Timothy. Only the Pastoral Epistles will reflect on this further. Finally, in the first New Testament phase it is also striking that Paul himself never mentions 'presbyters'. However, in certain church communities presbyteral order is very old. After the Twelve, in Jerusalem it was above all James, 'the brother of the Lord', who was revered as the great leader; but he was surrounded by a college of presbyters (following the pattern of the Jewish synagogue). He and these presbyters made important decisions for the community (Acts 11.30; 21.28; see 15.2). Presbyteral church order was later to spread widely from Jerusalem and then from the community in Rome.

2. The ministry in the post-apostolic biblical period

(a) 'On the foundation of the apostles and prophets'; new forms of ministry (Eph. 2.20; 4.7–16)

Only after the disappearance of the first generation, above all the apostles and prophets, did the theological problem of the ministry explicitly present itself to all communities (i.e. roughly between AD 80 and AD 100). Paul himself had in fact been intensely preoccupied with this problem shortly before his death (Phil. 2.19–24). This is precisely the time in which the ministry not only took on specific, albeit still changing features, but at the same time became the object of theological reflection, though people were less interested in actual structures of ministry.

The first founders of the communities had died; what was to be done next? On closer inspection, the use of pseudonyms or *noms de plume* – which at an earlier time was often interpreted in a rather unfavourable light – gives us a positive insight into this problem. At a time when the local leaders had lost the great bearers of their traditions and the pioneers in their community: Paul, Peter, James, a certain John, and so on, they could best 'legitimate' their own leadership to their fellow-Christians by stressing that they were simply carrying on the work, the gospel, of the apostles and prophets, those who founded the community and gave it life. When these leaders then in turn wrote letters to their communities, they did so in the name of the apostle who was the great traditional figure of their community. For example, the letter to Ephesus and the Pastoral Epistles are written as though they came personally from the apostle Paul. But the theology of 'the Pauline ministry' which they contain makes it clear that they represent post-Pauline reflection on what Paul in fact proposed: they are along the lines of Paul's own self-understanding. Precisely for that reason, the letters were written in the name of Paul. This custom of pseudonymity, widespread throughout the ancient world,[11] makes the basic intention of these letters all the clearer: the letters seek to carry on the 'apostolic tradition'; they build on the apostolic foundation which Paul had laid. So too in the Letter of Peter: probably a certain Silvanus (I Peter 5.12), who himself had formerly been one of Paul's fellow workers (I Thess. 1.1; Acts 15.40; 18.5), is writing his letter in the name of Peter, because this community is in the apostolic line deriving from Peter. And since Silvanus also had a personal predilection for Paul, we also find in this tradition an attempt to harmonize Paul and Peter (II Peter 3.15f.).

Thus pseudonymity conceals a whole theology of the ministry which has been thematized in one way or another in these same letters. This is already clear in the Deutero-Pauline letter to the Christians of Ephesus. In this letter, which is post-apostolic, but still in the New Testament, the theology of the ministry is central, at least as a background. Eph. 4.7–16 (which perhaps falls into two parts, Eph. 4.7–10 and 4.11–16) contains part of a theology of the ministry in which we can clearly see the transition from the apostolic to the post-apostolic period. After the death of the 'apostles and prophets', who are now called the foundation of the church (Eph. 2.20), the leaders of the community, here called 'evangelists, pastors and teachers' (Eph. 4.11; cf. 2.20 and 3.5), must continue to build on this foundation. Pastors and teachers seem to have been the local leaders, whereas evangelists were missionaries or delegates sent out by the community. Henceforward these post-apostolic leaders of communities were characterized by two indivisible qualifications. On the one hand, like the apostles (I Cor. 4.1; Rom. 10.14f., 17), they work in the name of Christ and are in his service. However, the new development compared with the first Christian generation is that on the other hand those who hold office in the church know that they are under obligation to the apostolic heritage (Paul had already said something like this: his fellow workers are bound to the foundation that he had laid, I Cor. 3.5–15). In the name and the service of Jesus Christ, they feel themselves responsible for the apostolicity of the community, because here they are given the guarantee that they truly remain 'communities of Jesus'. This was at the same time a period in which particular Christians, forgetting their historical origin, engaged in vigorous 'speculation', affected as they were by the syncretistic atmosphere of those days. The historical significance of the stress in the post-apostolic period on the apostolic heritage thus amounted to a reference to original experiences of real people who had arrived at a surprising new life through their encounter with Jesus. In the wake of the apostles, apostolicity points to the distinguishing mark of the community as being discipleship of Jesus. The post-apostolic leaders have to be concerned for this apostolic origin of Christian experience, from which the communities have to live from now on; in other words, for Christian identity. Their ministry – now the church's ministry – is thus experienced as a special ministerial charisma in the service of the community.

However, at the beginning of this transitional period the church's ministry was in no way detached from the community or so to speak set above it; ministry is clearly incorporated into the totality of all kinds of services which are necessary for the community (Eph. 4.11). The peculiarity of this ministerial charisma is that the ministers and the whole of the community have the responsibility for keeping the community in its apostolicity or apostolic origin and orientation: the gospel of Jesus the Christ. Moreover, it is the task of the ministers (though here another interpretation is also possible, depending on how the

Greek sentence is punctuated) 'to equip the saints (= Christians) for the work of ministry' (Eph. 4.12). If we end this clause after 'pastors and teachers', then as ministers these are also concerned with co-ordinating and encouraging all forms of service in the community. In any case, all forms of service, whether or not they are forms of official ministry, must be directed towards 'building up the body of the Lord' (Eph. 4.12b). Of course the tendency which is perceptible in the period between I Cor. 12.28ff. and the Deutero-Pauline Eph. 4.7–16 moves in the direction of stressing the service of the ministers in the church over against those which are not connected with the ministry (cf. also Eph. 4.7–16 with Col. 2.19).

Proclamation, leadership and building up the community in accordance with its apostolic foundation: this is unmistakably the theology of the ministry in Ephesians. Ephesians does not say how these ministers are appointed; how one became a leader of the community was not as yet a problem: it was a purely incidental matter. Of course ministers were called on to preserve the apostolicity of the communities, which had to remain 'communities of God' or 'of Jesus'. Here it was the requirement of apostolicity, rather than the mode of appointment, which was theologically relevant.

Does this view, above all of the ministry in the form of the presbyterate, go back to Paul himself? Presbyteral church order was unknown in the Syrian capital of Antioch, whose Christian community sent out Paul and Barnabas, their original leader. There is mention only of 'prophets and teachers' (Acts 13.1). However, Barnabas came to this already established community from Jerusalem, where there had long been a presbyteral church order. Now where Acts uses the term 'presbyter' in a Christian connection, we seem to have an element of the tradition which antedates Luke. In six places presbyters are mentioned alongside the original apostles, albeit exclusively in connection with the Apostolic Council (Acts 15.2, 4, 6, 22f.; 16.4). In Acts 11.30 there is mention only of presbyters who, according to Acts 21.18, assemble around James in order to hear Paul's report of the state of affairs. However, there are only two mentions of presbyters in Acts outside Jerusalem, in Asia Minor (14.23, for Lycaonia and Phrygia, and 20.17 for Ephesus). Now in Acts 14.23, Luke says that Barnabas and Paul appointed presbyters during their first missionary journey from Derbe in Lycaonia to the southern coast of Asia Minor. There have been arguments over the historicity of this account for over a century.[12] On the one hand people refer to the fact that the authentic letters of

Paul know nothing of presbyteral church order; on the other it is argued that apart from Galatians, no authentic letters of Paul are addressed to communities in Asia Minor, whereas according to Acts this is precisely the place where presbyteral church order was well known and in existence in about five local communities. Historically it cannot be denied that in the time of Luke the presbyterate was very widespread, outside Jerusalem above all in Asia Minor and in Crete (see I Tim.; Titus; I Peter). We can understand Acts 20.17 if we remember that the Christian community in Ephesus was not founded by Paul but by unknown Jewish Christians, which may explain the presence of the presbyteral church order there. In Acts 20.28 Luke wants to identify the unknown term *episcopos* with the well-known term presbyter; he is thus connecting two traditions. Moreover, there is a connection between the Christian presbyter and the Jewish institution of the synagogue presbyter (see Acts 14.23). (Furthermore, there were presbyteral dignitaries in the pagan temples of Asia Minor.) Given that Barnabas – who at that time was still the leader of the mission from Antioch to Asia Minor – came from Jerusalem, there is every reason to suppose that he brought the presbyteral model from Jerusalem to Asia Minor. Thus Acts 14.22f. does not in any way need to be regarded as unhistorical.

Historically, it can no longer be denied that towards the end of the first century there was a church order according to which a group of 'presbyters' was responsible for the leadership and pastoral care of the local communities (see Acts 14.23; 20.17, 20–30; I Peter 5.1; I Tim. 3.1–7; 5.17–22; Titus 1.5–11; James 5.14; II John 1.1; III John 1.1; also in the extra-canonical literature: I Clement 44; Didache 15.1). The presbyters are also called '*episcopoi*' without any perceptible difference, among other reasons because they had the function of oversight (*episcopē*).[13] Furthermore, the difference between prophetic preachers and teachers is also extremely small. In I Tim. 5.17 presbyters who not only preached but also taught seem to be held in double esteem. Some scholars rightly suppose all kinds of shifts in the meaning of the term 'presbyter', which as time went on increasingly took over the content of the earlier prophets and teachers. This shift is evident in the Didache. It speaks of 'prophets and teachers' (13.1f.; 15.2), but the difference is small and obscure, since the prophet also teaches (Didache 11.10f.), just as the difference between apostle and prophet (11.3–6) is also fluid because it is said of an apostle who stays too long in a community (at the community's expense) that he is a false 'prophet'.

Perhaps the only difference between prophet and teacher is that the prophet is a non-residential teacher (Didache 10.7–11.1), so that there is not always a prophet in the community (Didache 13.4). Thus in the Didache 'prophet' does not have, or no longer has, the significance of predominantly ecstatic enthusiasm, but that of teaching in word and deed. It is precisely this content of prophesying and teaching which was taken up into the term 'presbyter' when some degree of institutionalization developed in various communities.

(b) The Pastoral Epistles; I Peter; James

The Pastoral Epistles, I Peter and James, in different ways already sketch out for us some clear contours of this institutionalization of the church's ministry.

For the Pastoral Epistles Paul is the great bearer of the tradition in whose footsteps the community means to tread. Thus at one point the ministry of the church is even presented as an explicit institution made by Paul himself, since there it is Paul himself who lays hands on the presbyters (II Tim. 1.6), in contrast to I Tim. 5.22 (see I Tim. 4.14, and remember what is said about Barnabas in Acts 14.22f.). In these Pauline churches, henceforth certain Christians, in whom the community sees a charisma from the Lord, are appointed, instituted to the ministry by presbyters or local leaders who are already present. This happens through laying on of hands[14] by a college of presbyters and a word from a prophet (the later *epiclesis* at all consecrations). Thus in these later Pauline communities the feeling developed that the continuance of the leadership of the apostolic community, or the church, by ministers should also be secured in an institutional form. Although the community itself is also responsible for its apostolicity and precisely for this reason also has responsibility for the choice of its leaders on the grounds that here its own authenticity in terms of the gospel is at stake, the special function of the leaders of the community (in whatever form) is nevertheless brought more into relief. Because of the importance of this task, all kinds of criteria for admission are established (I Tim. 3.1–13); this is a kind of ethics and spirituality of the ministry. Although subject to these criteria, however, all Christians have the right 'to aspire to this office' (I Tim. 3.1). The post-apostolic leaders of the communities themselves clearly formulated their own self-understanding: they wanted to walk in the footsteps of the apostles and prophets. Hence we read in the superscriptions of the Pastoral

Epistles: 'Paul to Titus – to Timothy – his true child in the common faith' (Titus 1.4; see I Tim. 1.2; see already Paul himself: I Thess. 3.2; I Cor. 4.17; I Cor. 16.10; Phil. 2.22; II Cor. 7.6, 13, 14). Both Timothy and Titus (clearly ministers of the church, though never called *'episcopos'* or *'presbyteros'*) are called 'true children' of the apostolic faith in order to stress the legitimacy of their ministry. The qualification 'true' is added with good reason: their faith is built on the apostolic heritage, and therefore they are the authentic guarantee of the apostolicity of the communities.

Thus in the Pastoral Epistles the ministry is not formally, as such, a norm; the norm is the *paratheke*, the 'pledge entrusted' (I Tim. 6.20, which also ends the letter, and II Tim. 1.14, which also begins it). In II Tim. 1.10–14 we are told the specific content of this deposit which is entrusted to Paul, viz. the gospel (1.11; see also II Tim. 2.8), as the apostles have interpreted it. The Pastoral Epistles call this interpreted gospel the *didaskalia*, the teaching (I Tim. 1.10; II Tim. 4.3; Titus 1.9; 2.1 etc.). In Titus 2.10 we therefore find the phrase 'the *didaskalia* of God our Saviour'. For these letters Paul is the great *didaskalos* or teacher of this divine gospel (I Tim. 2.7; II Tim. 1.11). The Pastoral Epistles thus show (following what Paul himself had said about Timothy and Titus) a special interest in the continuity of the apostolic tradition, the main theme of these three letters. Primarily the concern is quite definitely not so much with an unbroken succession or continuity in the ministry as with an unbroken succession in teaching, in the apostolic tradition. II Timothy 2.2 states this explicitly: 'The teaching which you have heard from me before many witnesses entrust to faithful men who will be able to teach others also.' The succession in question here is clearly that of the apostolic gospel: Paul receives it from God (I Tim. 1.11: Paul himself spoke of himself and his fellow workers as *theou synergoi*, fellow workers with God, I Cor. 3.9); for his part Paul hands it down to Titus and Timothy (I Tim. 6.20; II Tim. 1.13f.), and these must in turn hand on the same liberating gospel to trustworthy Christians, ministers in the church (II Tim. 2.2). Thus the focal point is clearly handing on intact the apostolic gospel, 'the pledge entrusted'. The ministry as a service is subordinate to this continuity or succession which is apostolic in content; there must always be ministry in the church for the sake of continuity. Ministry is necessary for the sake of the gospel. Paul himself had already said, 'How are men to believe in him of whom they have never heard? And how are they to hear without a preacher?' (Rom. 10.14). For this reason different commentators have rightly said that in the Pastoral Epistles the central feature is not the principle of the ministry, much less the structures of the ministry (which remain vague), but *the principle of the apostolic tradition*. This is expressed even in the rite of the laying on of hands, which these letters want to see introduced. For here, too, there is primarily no question of the transference of ministerial authority, but of the charisma of the Holy Spirit, which will help the minister to hand down and preserve in a living way the pledge entrusted to him and to make him able to proclaim the apostolic tradition intact (I Tim. 4.13f.; II Tim. 1.6, 14). Ministry is necessary, even qualified ministry (Titus 1.5–9), in order to keep the community on apostolic lines: 'the community of Jesus'.

What ministries are needed? The Pastoral Epistles do not seem to be interested in this; this falls outside the normative *didaskalia*. In fact, in the communities to which these letters are addressed there are already specific differentiations in ministry, but we can discover virtually nothing about the precise sphere of competence of each. Thus there are: 1. *deacons* (I Tim. 3.8–13; II Tim. 4.5), though we are never told what their function is. They are simply urged to be good and required to be *homines probati*, tested by the community (I Tim. 3.10); when anything is said about their work, this virtually coincides with what is said about the *episcopoi*. 2. In addition there is a college of *presbyteroi* (I Tim. 4.14), who 'preside' over or lead the community (I Tim. 5.17; Titus 1.5). Among them are evidently people who are active above all 'in the word and teaching' (I Tim. 5.17), the teachers or catechists of former times; this even seems to be a function which carries with it the right to recompense (I Tim. 5.17f.), although this last is a universal basic rule in the New Testament (see Matt. 10.10; I Cor. 9.1–18; II Cor. 11.7–11). We are nowhere told whether there were also 'presbyters' who did not preside and did not teach. 3. Finally, two texts mention an *overseer* or *episcopos* (I Tim. 3.2; Titus 1.7). It is also said of him that he 'teaches and directs' (Titus 1.9; I Tim. 3.2). Is the *episcopos* a *presbyteros*, perhaps head of the presbyteral team? What specific function does he perform? These letters give us no information on such questions. They are evidently not at all interested in the specific structure of the ministry.[15] It is here that we find the great difference from the interest which will develop later, e.g. already in the letters of Ignatius, in which the structures of the ministry occupy a central place, and the spheres of authority are well defined in terms of church order.[16] Furthermore, in clear contrast to the Pastoral

Epistles, I Clement (42.4, 5, compared with 44.1f.) already calls
the office of *presbyteros-episcopos* a divine institution. By contrast,
the Pastoral Epistles do not give us any norm whatsoever as to
how the ministry must in fact be structured and differentiated;
they simply say that the ministry is needed to preserve in a
living way the apostolicity of the community's tradition. Only
this last point is theologically relevant; giving it specific form is
thus evidently a pastoral question, which the church must consider afresh on each occasion.[17] Through the introduction of the
laying on of hands (above all after the disappearance of the
prophets from the church), these letters obviously want to ensure that there is always a ministry in the church. This laying
on of hands, with prayer, is therefore an institution of the
church and makes a great deal of sense (later it is a canonical
obligation), but we can hardly appeal to the New Testament
and to dogma in order to make it a *sine qua non* for all time of
the way in which the ministry is actually to function in the
church. The building up of the community undergoes further
historical development, in apostolic continuity, even after the
first and second scriptural phases.

In the Letter of James the presbyteral church order is taken
for granted. 'Is any among you sick? Let him call for the elders
of the church, and let them pray over him, anointing him with
oil in the name of the Lord' (James 5.14).

For the New Testament period, we can say that from Jerusalem and, somewhat later, from Rome, presbyteral church
order replaced the undifferentiated church order of the first
period throughout early Christianity, also and even above all in
the Pauline communities. I Peter is typical of the disappearance
of the undifferentiated, charismatic type of church in which
'prophets and teachers' were the most prominent figures, in
favour of the institution of a presbyteral leadership of the
church. It was probably written from the community of Rome
to churches in Asia Minor, on the eve of a persecution of the
church there (perhaps under the emperor Domitian). In I
Peter 1.1–4.11 there is clear mention of a charismatic origin of
ministries, but in the second part of this letter, from I Peter 5.1–
5 on, there is an unmistakable mention of a presbyteral church
order. Here the two types of church still stand side by side.
However, in a situation of possible church persecution (I
Peter 4.14–16), the writer still sees salvation and preservation
for the threatened community in the introduction of a strict,
presbyteral church order, although this college of pastors is
subject to the norm of the 'arch-pastor, Jesus' (I Peter 5.4). In

the letter written at about the same time by the presbyter Clement from Rome to the community in Corinth, the increasing pressure to introduce presbyteral church order everywhere is clearly perceptible. In Corinth a schism had arisen between the charismatic 'office-bearers' and the supporters of a more institutional, presbyteral order. Clement intervenes and obliges the community to introduce the presbyteral church order (I Clement 44.1ff); he himself will be sending a delegation to establish whether the community has been obedient in this respect (I Clement 65.1). We must therefore note that there is a clearly uniform development in the direction of a presbyteral church order between Acts 20.28 (see also 14.23); II Tim. 3.1; I Peter 5.1–5 and I Clement 44.1ff. It would be a good thing to add here that, in view of the importance of the church's ministry for preserving Christian identity, at that time above all over against 'gnostic' errors, interest in the other charismata in the community (which was constantly maintained by Paul) almost completely disappears in the Pastoral Epistles and many post-apostolic writings of the New Testament. Without moving in the direction of conservatism, given the threat of persecution and heretical errors, the Pastoral Epistles above all clearly have the beginnings of an obsession with the teaching ministry as the only means of preserving the Christian identity. Paul's trust in the Spirit which dwells in the whole of the Christian community, leads it and carries it along (shaken though it often was by the community) is hardly present at all in the Pastoral Epistles. At that time people did not yet have the experience of later centuries, when 'Christendom' was filled with amazement because most of those who held office (at that time already bishops) prized the Arian heresy, while the believing people rescued the church's orthodoxy!

(c) Matthaean community leaders

There is no evidence anywhere in the New Testament that there were communities without any ministry. In addition to the founders of communities, above all, prophets and teachers were at work everywhere. However, it is quite another question whether at that time ministry always took the institutional form of the presbyterate.

In addition, for example, to the Corinthian communities, where there is no mention of presbyters, we see something of this kind especially in the so-called Matthaean communities. Already in the Gospel of Matthew it is stressed that in the community (which understands itself as a brotherhood in which all differences of rank and status have disappeared) no one may call himself 'rabbi, teacher or father' (Matt. 23.8–10); Jesus alone is the teacher of the communities (Matt. 23.8). However, fundamentally this is the view of all the primitive Christian communities. Even Paul's apostolate was a *diakonia* or service, not a matter of ruling (II Cor. 1.24; I Cor. 3.5; Rom. 11.13; II Cor. 3.3–9; 4.1; 5.18; 6.3f.); it is above all 'a ministry of reconciliation' (II Cor. 5.18; see II Cor. 3.4–6). Throughout the New Testament ministry is nowhere conceived of as a structure in accordance with the worldly model of 'leadership', in the sense of rulers being over subjects. On the contrary, as all three synoptics say (Mark 10.42f.; Luke 22.25; Matt. 20.25f.), 'It shall not be so (as is the case with worldly rulers) among you'.

Throughout the New Testament leadership is service or *diakonia* (I Cor. 16.15f.; 12.28; II Cor. 3.7–9; 4.1; 5.18; 6.3; II Tim. 4.5; Eph. 4.11f.; Col. 4.17). The same thing applies even when the presbyteral ministry of leadership comes more into prominence: 'I exhort the presbyters among you. . .tend the flock of God of which you are the pastors; keep it in accordance with God's will: from the heart and not under constraint, with dedication and not from the desire for gain. Do not domineer over those who are entrusted to your care, but be an example for the flock' (I Peter 5.1–4).[18] Thus the particularity of Matthew cannot lie here. Of course, like all the earliest Christian communities, his gospel is familiar with 'prophets and teachers' or 'wise men' (see Matt. 5.12; 7.22; 10.41; 11.25; 13.52; 23.8–10, 34). However, it is striking that the Gospel of Matthew is very cautious, and issues polemic against 'false prophets' (7.15f.) and 'false teachers' (5.18f.), which presupposes the authentic functions of prophet and teacher. But Matthew wants a community 'of the little' (*mikroi* is a key word throughout his gospel), and this subjects the actual practice of leading the community, above all in the way of the world, to severe criticism. This is connected with Matthew's view of the church, whose members are 'sons of the kingdom of God' (Matt. 13.38), but still under the proviso of the judgment (Matt. 25.31–46); this is a church 'made up of good and evil' (22.10; see 13.36–43; 18.7). Matthew will not tolerate 'office bearers' whose conduct is not in accord with the kingdom of God: Matthew is concerned with 'the kingdom of God and his righteousness' (Matt. 6.33), i.e. the kingdom of God and the life-style which conforms to this kingdom, and this last is revealed in actions with fellow human beings (Matt. 7.21–23; 25.31–46). Matthew goes on to depict both the good and the weak sides of the immediate disciples of Jesus; they are paradigmatic types of all Christians, the Christians in Matthew's own community: believers, certainly, but above all 'of little faith' (Matt. 6.30; 8.26; 14.31; 16.8; 17.20). The way in which Peter is typified points in the same direction (Matt. 4.18; 10.2; 14.28–31; 16.17–19, 24–27; 18.21f.); here Peter is the prototype of the community leader, the first, the spokesman for the whole community (16.18f.; 20.20–27, with perhaps a 'monarchical' tendency in this form of church order). Following the lines of the Q tradition, Matthew also states that the disciple is not above the master (Matt. 10.24f.); being a follower of Jesus involves bearing the cross (10.17–25; 16.21–28; 20.22f.). Thus Matthew expresses a special form of criticism of the ministry because he is critical of the church, which still stands under the eschatological proviso. However, this gospel is probably subject to the teaching authority of Peter.

At all events, the Gospel of Matthew points to the existence of a still free, earlier system of 'prophets and teachers' – and does not seem to be familiar with presbyteral church orders; so this freer system seems to have existed longer in some areas of the Syrian churches than in many other Christian communities. Of course this freer, charismatic system of 'prophets and teachers' had many disadvantages for a developing church, particularly in conflict with false teachings. The Didache, itself closely related to the Matthaean tradition, is particularly important here. It is generally accepted that this 'Didache of the Apostles' falls into two parts, written at different times (Didache 1.1–11.2; 11.3–16.8). This document speaks of 'apostles' (11.4–6), 'prophets' (11.7–12) and 'teachers' (13.2), and the author is principally concerned to distinguish the authentically charismatic office-holders from false apostles, prophets and teachers, who are motivated by the desire for gain. We find the early Christian titles, apostles, prophets, teachers (I Cor. 12.28), clearly enough here; following the line of Eph. 2.20, apostles and prophets belong together in a special way (Didache 11.4–12). 'Apostles' here in no way refers to the old first apostles, but to those holding office in contemporary 'Didache communities'. Their task is *kerygma* (the proclamation of the gospel) and *didache* (interpreting the gospel for present circumstances). In addition to their ordinary and extraordinary (perhaps 'apocalyptic') teachings, the prophets also seem to have their own function at the breaking of the bread and the eucharistic celebration which follows (Didache 11.9, in connection with chs. 9 and 10). The community is required to be able to distinguish between true and false prophets and teachers (11.7–12, which also suggests the exercise of a charismatic ministry). The teachers share with the prophets 'the ministry of the word', though here the teachers do not seem to enjoy the same prestige as the prophets (in the Letter of Barnabas, which has an affinity with the Didache, the teaching of the prophets is distinguished more precisely from that of the teachers: Barn. 18.1). After this exposition Didache 15.1f. suddenly says, '*Thus* choose *episcopoi* and *diakonoi* worthy of the Lord. . .for they too fulfil the ministry of prophets and teachers among you;. . .they are among your prominent figures, along with the prophets and teachers.' This clearly points to later, changed circumstances in the Didache communities. In fact, in Didache 9 and 10 the writer had described the whole of the liturgy of the breaking of the bread and the subsequent celebration of the eucharist (in which prophets preside: 'let the prophets celebrate the eucharist as they will', Didache 10.7). However, it is evident from 14.1 that since then a change had been introduced into this service. Henceforth what we have is a weekly meeting on Sunday, followed by a eucharist, and moreover this is now preceded by a common, liturgical penitential celebration. For this reason ('thus', says Didache 14.1), each community must choose overseers (*episkopoi*) and helpers (*diakonoi*) – how, is not said – so that this more frequent and extended celebration of the eucharist may be prepared for in an orderly way, and may be carried out properly. Thus the *episkopoi* and their helpers are here at the service of the prophets (and teachers) who (continue to) preside at this liturgy; these newcomers share in the liturgical leadership or in the ministry of these prophets and teachers. For that reason, 'they too must be held in honour (by the community) in the same way as the prophets and teachers' (Didache 15.1f.). Thus in these communities at least the ministry of *episcopoi* and *diakonoi* is introduced to take some burdens from the prophets and teachers who lead the community (with all that this involves). So here we have a quite different context for new ministries from what we find, for example, in the introduction of presbyteral church order in I Clement, written to the Christians of Corinth.

Consequently, even after the New Testament, church order remains very varied in the different communities. The fact that the Didache emphatically points out that overseers and helpers must be held in as much respect in the community as the prophets and teachers perhaps points towards a certain restraint on the part of these communities towards these new ministries.

In these communities of a Matthaean type the old order
(prophets and teachers) was clearly of longer standing than
presbyters, and there was even a degree of animosity towards
the (later) introduction of *episcopoi* and *diakonoi*. The so-called
Apocalypse of Peter (from the same line of tradition) later issues
sharp polemic against the new institutional form of church order
in the ministry. However, on the other hand it is striking that
all the communities of this more charismatic type disappeared
completely in the course of the second century, or fell victim to
Christian Gnostic sects.

In historical terms, it emerges from this situation that a community without a good, matter-of-fact pastoral institutionalization of its ministry (a development of it in changed
circumstances) runs the risk of losing for good the apostolicity
and thus ultimately the Christian character of its origin, inspiration and orientation – and in the last resort its own identity.
Ministry is connected with a special concern for the preservation
of the Christian identity of the community in constantly changing circumstances. Paul already says, 'All things are lawful, but
not all things are helpful.' This is the lesson to be learned from
the history of the 'Matthaean communities', which evidently
defended in a one-sided way the charismatic approach against
any institutionalization of it. The historical information we can
discover about these communities must also make us ask
whether the Great Church, which was in fact becoming
world-wide, left sufficient room for those communities which
did not follow a Pauline direction, and seem to have continued
to look for all salvation from a purely charismatic leadership in
the ministry through the spirit. As a result they were forced to
the periphery of the Great Church, which was in the process of
becoming an institution. This history should therefore teach us
a twofold lesson: the dangerous and creative recollection of the
necessary unity in tension between charisma and its institutionalization. Ministry without charisma becomes starved and
threatens to turn into a power institution; charisma without any
institutionalization threatens to be volatilized into fanaticism
and pure subjectivity, quickly becoming the plaything of opposing forces, to the detriment of the apostolic communities. So
the stress is placed by the post-apostolic churches of the New
Testament on the apostolicity of the communities, which ask
for ministers; that is an essentially Christian intuition.

(d) Johannine community leaders

The Johannine communities had to learn a similar historical lesson. Commentators pass very different verdicts on the ministry in these churches. According to E. Schweizer and others,[19] there were no structures of ministry here, far less particular charismata of individual believers. Left to the Fourth Gospel alone, we would have to say that in this Gospel the existence of the ministry is neither denied or confirmed; we simply hear nothing about it. However, the Johannine Epistles from the same milieu are clearly thoroughly familiar with the presbyteral ministry (II John 1.1; III John 1). In the meanwhile more precise studies have made it clear that while the Johannine communities were familiar with a structured ministry, this was a ministry without any claim to authority, to such a degree that to begin with Johannine theology was opposed to authority in teaching and discipline being invested in the ministry. This was in contrast to other Christian communities. For this very reason, the structure of the ministry in Johannine theology is strongly relativized. For these communities, a direct and personal bond with Jesus was determinative for Johannine ecclesiology or the doctrine of the church. The consequences of this for their conception of the ministry emerge clearly.

The Fourth Gospel is, of course, on the one hand familiar with the group of the Twelve (John 6.70); however, it is striking that in contrast to the Synoptic Gospels it does not give any list of twelve names, nor does it have any account of the calling of the Twelve. On the other hand, in II and III John there is mention of 'the presbyter', a community leader who writes these letters. For some commentators this is the most important presbyter,[20] and the community tends towards a mono-episcopal church order, but this is difficult to reconcile with the collective witness given by these letters (see below). Others look in the direction of the notions of the presbyter to be found in Papias and Irenaeus,[21] but according to these last the presbyters teach with authority; here presbyters were the generation of teachers who came after the eyewitnesses and taught with authority because they derived this authority through their link, as immediate successors, with those who had themselves seen and heard Jesus. However, in Johannine theology the presbyters simply had no authority. This is connected with the doctrine of the church and the Spirit in these communities. Here the Paraclete is regarded as the only teacher (John 14.26; 16.13); the human teachers, even 'the beloved disciple' (the bearer of the tradition of these communities) are simply witnesses of the tradition which was interpreted by the Paraclete (19.35; 21.24; I John 2.27). After the death of the beloved disciple these communities understand that the work of the Paraclete is continued by the followers of the beloved disciple who had handed down the tradition to them.[22] The presbyter of the second and third letter thus speaks as a member of a collective 'we' which bears witness of what has been seen and heard in the beginning (I John 1.1f.). Here, at any rate, this collective 'we' is not the whole of the Johannine community (as is the case in other texts in I John), but a group of those who interpret and hand down the tradition and who address the communities as 'you' – the little children (I John 1.1–5; cf. the 'we' of John 21.24 with I John 1.1f.). This presbyter speaks as a long-lived representative of the Johannine school; he can say, 'What *we* have seen and heard from the beginning', not because he himself was an eyewitness but because he knows himself to be close to the school of the disciples of the beloved disciple. The continuity of links in this one chain becomes clear: Jesus saw God; the beloved disciple saw Jesus; the Johannine school shares in this tradition. M. de Jonge rightly says that the *pluralis apostolicus* goes over into a *pluralis ecclesiasticus* which is, however, incomprehensible without the *pluralis apostolicus*.[23] When the Gospel of John was written, the witness of the beloved disciple was enough (John 19.35; 21.24). However, when the Johannine letters were written, the situation in the Johannine communities had changed. Two parties in conflict with one another claimed to be the authentic interpreters of the one tradition of the beloved disciple. As a member of the Johannine school 'the presbyter' (who writes these letters) tries to convince his opponents of their deviation from this great tradition. He cannot do more than this, because he can only bear witness and cannot speak with authority; at all events, the Johannine Christians have no need to be taught by men (I John 2.27); that is what false prophets do (I John 4.1). The opponents of the writer of the letter probably called themselves 'prophets and teachers'. Was this also the earlier form of Johannine church order, as, for example, in the Matthaean communities? Or was this simply the situation of the secessionist opponents? At all events, the concept of the Paraclete who is always at work (John 14.16) relativizes both the delay of the parousia and the significance of the ministry in the church. For Johannine theology it is never such a bad thing that Jesus went away, for at Easter he would return in the Paraclete (John 16.7), who teaches all things (14.26) in truth (16.13). The Spirit itself bears witness along with the witness of the Johannine believers (15.26f.). This is typically Johannine. The chrism or anointing of I John 2.20, 27, the gift of Christ to all believers, is not a charisma of enthusiasm and ecstasy but a capacity, given through the Spirit, for all believers to interpret the (Johannine) tradition faithfully.

However, according to I John 3.24–4.6, 13, in conflicts it is necessary to test this spiritual interpretation. According to I John 5.6–8 the criterion here is that the witness of the Spirit is bound up with the witness at the baptism in the Jordan (water) and at the death of Jesus (blood) – clearly directed against the Johannine secessionists. I John thus stresses what the Gospel of John had to some extent left in the background, namely that Jesus himself is the Paraclete (John 14.16 speaks of 'the *other* Paraclete'). The only reference in I John to the Paraclete is I John 2.1f., and here Jesus himself is called Paraclete, viz. in his function as the one who speaks for us to the Father and the one who atones for sin. Following the line taken by the Fourth Gospel, in reaction against opponents I John wants to connect the Paraclete even more strongly with Jesus, who is 'from above'. This writer-presbyter identifies the Paraclete with the 'pneumatic Christ' and thus with Jesus of Nazareth who appeared on earth, was baptized in the water of the Jordan and glorified on the cross.

In contrast to both Pauline theology and the Matthaean communities, in which error is countered with an authoritative statement by the apostle Paul or later by the presbyters, or by Peter, the Johannine presbyter does not seem to have this authority; here the Paraclete is the only authoritative teacher, and he is given to all believers without exception. This relativizes the ministry of the presbyters (moreover, even the beloved disciple is never called 'apostle': he is not one of the Twelve, and even after his death there is no need to replace him: see John 21.20–23).

It emerges from all this that the Johannine presbyter is unable to correct his opponents by the authority of his office. In Johannine terms, he can only refer to the inner leading of the Holy Spirit (I John 2.20): 'you all (*pantes*, not the variant reading *panta*) have knowledge' (see also I John 2.27, to be compared with John 14.26). The authority of the presbyter lies in his collegial membership of the 'we' as an instrument of the Spirit: they, the secessionists, have disrupted this community. Therefore this presbyter can only seek a test from the Holy Spirit to see who is right here and who are the false prophets (I John 4.1–3). The criterion here is 'Jesus Christ, who has come in the flesh' (I John 4.2f.; cf. I John 4.6). The secessionists in no way deny the earthly Jesus, nor do they transfigure him in docetic fashion, but they do deny the saving significance of the earthly Jesus, and above all the saving significance of his death. However, as a good representative of Johannine theology the presbyter knows that such a testing is of little use, since 'the world' (and that is the Johannine secessionists: I John 4.5; II John 7) listens to opponents (I John 4.5). For Johannine theology worldly success is a contra-indication for Christianity (John 3.19; 14.17; 15.18f.; 16.8–10; 17.23, 26; I John 2.9, 18).

In III John the church situation has become even worse. Here the presbyter is in conflict with another Johannine presbyter, Diotrephes. In this conflict we can see clear signs of two divergent views of authority[24] in connection with the question raised on each side: How can we best preserve Christians from error? (For each of the two presbyters the other is the false teacher.) The presbyter sends a delegation to bear witness before Diotrephes to the true tradition (III John 5–8, 12). He does not have the authority to depose Diotrephes; he can only refer to the inner worth of the witness and thus simply challenge Diotrephes (III John 10). However, for the other, the delegation consists of false prophets. Diotrephes, presumably the leader of one of the many Johannine house communities, is thus confronted with the problem of good and false prophets (here the situation is the same as it was in Matthew and in Didache 11). However, of his own accord he decides not to receive those who in his view are false prophets. For the presbyter of III John this is an abuse of the status of presbyter: Diotrephes allows his interpretation of the Johannine tradition to be the highest authority and so 'puts himself first' (III John 9). In other words, here a church leader, in opposition to the Johannine ethos, has taken a step towards 'the authority of the ministry', as this was accepted in most non-Johannine communities. III John protests against this.

If the additional chapter, John 21, was written at about the same time as, above all, I John, some interesting consequences follow.[25] Here the fate of the beloved disciple is presented as part of a divine plan; he is in no way inferior to Peter, even though he does not die the death of a martyr. On the other hand, the author of John 21 commends Peter as an authority to his Johannine readers: he is in no way anti-Petrine. But about six texts in the Gospel of John (13.23; 18.15f.; 20.2–10; 21.7; 21.20–23; 19.26f.) show that Peter, the paradigm of the apostolic church, did not understand Jesus so thoroughly and so profoundly as the beloved disciple, the paradigm of the Johannine communities. John 21 indeed underlines the pastoral role and the authority of Peter over all the church, but after Peter has been subjected to the Johannine criterion of love (three times: John 21.15–17): the principle of the direct and personal bond, in Johannine theology, between each believer, even those in authority, and Jesus. This then become the basis of all pastoral authority in the church, just as in the end Johannine theology is forced by the situation to accept it. Here is a symbolic description of two forms of church (for the beloved disciple is not himself assigned the role of an authority, as is Peter). Only in John 21 do the Johannine communities accept the full 'authority of the ministry', at least as founded on the personal bond in love to the one norm Jesus Christ.

Thus in Johannine theology there is certainly a structure of ministry, but to begin with this was in no way a teaching authority. Only gradually does Johannine theology arrive at the experience that a mere reference to the anointing of each believer with the Spirit (I John 2.27) is insufficient to keep the community true to the gospel. John 21, above all, is witness to the fact that in the end even the Johannine church accepts the authority of ministers in teaching and discipline, but nevertheless makes these church structures relative: the picture of the vine and the branches, i.e. a direct and personal bond with Jesus (a theme which marks the whole of the Fourth Gospel) remains the basis for all church authority as well. For the whole of Johannine Christianity the primary thing is the living presence of Jesus in every Christian, thanks to the indwelling of the Paraclete. As canonical writing, therefore, the Johannine corpus is a biblical admonition against any legalistic garb for church authority. After the Johannine Epistles we find no further sign of Johannine communities in the second century; they were taken up into the apostolic Great Church or slipped over into gnostic sects. In the 'Great Church', church authority exercised by human beings became a sign of divine authority.[26]

3. Ministry and the building up of the community

(a) Pioneers in the community, and those who inspired it and served as models by which the community could identify the gospel

Throughout the development of the ministry in the New Testament one striking fact is that the ministry did not develop from and around the eucharist or the liturgy, but from the apostolic building up of the community through preaching, admonition and leadership.[27] No matter what different form it takes, ministry is concerned with the leadership of the community: ministers are pioneers, those who inspire the community and serve as models by which the whole community can identify the gospel. For the New Testament, there is evidently no special problem as to who should preside at the eucharist: we are told nothing directly in this connection. Furthermore, Paul does not call the eucharist an 'apostolic tradition' but a 'tradition of the Lord himself' (I Cor. 11.23), to which, therefore, even the apostles are bound. The eucharist is Jesus' parting gift to the whole community, which therefore has the right to it – the right by grace – regardless of all kinds of complicated problems over the ministry: 'Do this in remembrance of me.' Nowhere in the New Testament is an explicit connection made between the ministry of the church and presiding at the eucharist (except to some degree in Acts 13.1f.). However, that does not mean that any believer whatsoever could preside at the eucharist. In the house churches of Corinth it was the hosts who presided at the eucharistic meal, but these were at the same time leaders of the house churches. Thus this does not in any way imply that the eucharist was detached from the ministry.[28] On the other hand, there are no biblical grounds anywhere for a sacral and mystical foundation to the ministry in the eucharist. If we remember that the early eucharist was structured after the pattern of Jewish grace at meals – the *birkat hamazon* – at which not just anyone could preside,[29] it is evident that leaders of the community *ipso facto* also presided at the eucharist, and this is also evident from the texts written at the same time as the last part of the New Testament. In the earliest stratum of the Didache, the 'prophets and teachers' preside at the eucharist; in a later stratum they are joined by presbyters, who do so by virtue of their office.[30] In I Clement the president is the *episkopos*-presbyter. Thus the general conception is that anyone who is competent to lead the community in one way or another is *ipso facto* also president at the eucharist (and in this sense presiding at the eucharist does not need any separate authorization). The New Testament does not tell us more than this: later on we shall see how in the course of history the link between community and ministry is narrowed down to an inner bond between priesthood and eucharist.

According to the New Testament understanding, ministry is a constituent part of the church (apart from the question whether it is originally charismatic and then becomes institutionalized, and apart from the way in which it takes on different structures depending on the different needs of the church in changing circumstances). Ministry is necessary for building up the church along apostolic lines, viz., as the community of God, the apostolic discipleship of Jesus. Here the apostolic community with its apostolic heritage, viz., the gospel, takes a central place. The ministry is a service to this apostolicity and for these reasons can also itself be called apostolic, especially as a service to the apostolic community with its apostolic gospel. Thus it is apostolic not so much in the sense of an unbroken chain of apostolic succession in the ministry (which in view of the post-apostolic *ordinatio* has in fact become the actual form of church order), but first of all and in principle in the sense of the apostolicity of the gospel of the community, which also has the right to ministers who make sure that it remains in line with this apostolic origin. Therefore the minister is not merely a mouthpiece of the community, but occasionally can also reprimand it, just as on the other hand the community can also call its ministers to order. Precisely because the ministers are leaders and pioneers in the community, as 'the greatest' they must in fact be the least in the community: the principal servant of all (Mark 10.43f.). There is no mention in the New Testament of an essential distinction between 'laity' and 'ministers'. The particular character of the ministry is set against the background of many different, non-ministerial services in the church. In this sense the ministry is not a status, but in fact a function, though it is rightly called 'a gift of the Spirit' by the community *qua* assembly of God. For the New Testament, the essential apostolic structure of the community and therefore of the ministry of its leaders has nothing to do with what is called the 'hierarchical' structure of the church (on the basis of later Roman models in the Roman empire, and even later of feudal structures), except in a very inauthentic sense. It derives its own functions within the whole from what needs to happen within the church community. Ministry is not a status or *ordo* in the sense of the Roman senatorial *ordo* or status (although later people began to put it this way, and in particular to structure it accordingly). Because, on the other hand, the church is not concerned with civil ministry, but with service to a 'community of God', the ministry of the church above all requires of its ministers leadership in the true discipleship of Jesus, with all the spirituality which this 'discipleship of Jesus' involves in

New Testament terms. It is later said that the priest is *forma gregis*, the figure with whom the community identifies.

(b) Luke's 'Pauline testament' to community leaders

In Acts 20.17–38, Luke makes Paul summon the community leaders (here called presbyters) to him for his definitive farewell to his community in Ephesus. In the subsequent testament made by the apostle to the local community leaders who are following in his footsteps, Luke gives a good picture of the later New Testament conception of the ministry. Of course we can find many parallels to it elsewhere (e.g. in the Pastoral Epistles and in I Peter, but also already in Paul's authentic letters).

This testament can be summed up in five points.

1. After the death of the apostles and the other founders of communities, the ministry of leaders of the church is a gift of grace which they have received from the Lord (Acts 20.28: 'The flock in which the Holy Spirit has made you guardians, to feed the church of the Lord').

2. This service consists in bearing witness to 'the gospel of the grace of God' (Acts 20.24).

3. Like Paul, the minister is one who 'preaches the kingdom' (Acts 20.25): he must devote himself to the cause which Jesus espoused, the kingdom of God which becomes manifest in the action and life of the community as it is inaugurated in the message and the action of Jesus, in which this kingdom of God becomes the object of concrete experience.

4. This witness or 'martyrium' often also acquires the significance of a 'witness to death', as it did with Jesus and many of the apostles who were killed. The apostle, the minister, even the Christian, is not just the witness of Jesus' suffering (see I Peter 5.1f.), but also a witness by virtue of his own suffering (a tradition which can be found in Mark; in I Peter 5.1f.; in Hebrews; see also II Tim. 4.6f., and of course in many subsidiary New Testament traditions). Until well into the second century, 'the witness' or martyr, i.e. a Christian who had confessed Jesus as Christ before the civil authorities and as a result, according to Roman norms, was already guilty of a capital offence, *ipso facto* became an official witness to the apostolic tradition (regardless of whether he had actually had been executed). According to some documents from the second century this qualified him to be a church leader, an authentic witness to the apostolic tradition, if he was accepted by a community. When this happened, the confessor did not need any *ordinatio* or in-

stitution through the laying on of hands (which in the meanwhile had become obligatory, according to canon law).[31] Suffering and withstanding torture for the sake of faith in Jesus the Christ had 'consecrated' him as an authentic witness of the apostolic tradition; to put it in anachronistic terms: he had become a 'priest', a witness and guarantor of the apostolicity of the Christian community. The Christian who has suffered and been tested is thus the obvious candidate for the ministry. The Epistle to the Hebrews has made this a theme in terms of Jesus' own and unique priesthood. Although from a Jewish point of view Jesus was a layman, through his solidarity in suffering with his people he is a true high priest.[32]

5. In the spirit of Luke, who himself repeatedly was able to speak of Christian joy, we can add to this testament that according to the Pauline conception of the ministry, the minister is in the last resort someone who 'contributes to the joy (of the community)' (II Cor. 1.24). In any case, all who 'labour for the community' proclaim the message of reconciliation (II Cor. 5.18ff.): the joyful tidings of liberation and of a God who is concerned for mankind and for humaneness. Even in suffering, ministers are those who bring joy.

(c) The apostolicity of the community and the ministry

The preceding analyses of the conceptions of the ministry and the way in which it was put into practice in the New Testament churches now allow us to make a brief synthesis.

The New Testament shows that the early church was conscious of being apostolic. 'Apostolic' signifies in the first place the awareness of the Christian communities that they are built on the foundation of the 'apostles and prophets' of the earliest church. According to the New Testament, a living community is a community of believers who appropriate the cause of Jesus, i.e. the coming kingdom of God as essentially bound up with the whole of the career and ultimately the very person of Jesus, and therefore seek to maintain the story of and about Jesus in its significance for the future of all humanity. Here the accent lies not so much on a doctrine to be preserved in all possible purity – though that is also a factor – as on 'the story of and about Jesus', and 'the discipleship of Jesus', i.e. a Christian life-style, following Jesus, to be experienced in the most radical way possible, according to the orientation, the inspiration and the stimulus of 'the kingdom of God and his righteousness' (Matt. 6.33). This is the power of the love of a God concerned for humanity, the Christian dream as a force which will shape the future, 'Behold God's dwelling is with men' (Rev. 21.1–4). In essentials what we have here is an assembly of believers, a community in which the vision of the 'new heaven and the new earth' is kept alive with reference to Jesus of Nazareth, confessed as 'the Christ, God's only beloved Son, our Lord', and in prophetic witness and practice conformed to this kingdom of God.

This 'community of God' is a brotherhood in which the power structures prevailing in the world are broken down (Matt. 20.25f.; Luke 22.25; Mark 10.42f.): all are equal, though we might say that the lowly, the poor and the oppressed are more equal (to alter that well-known statement, 'all men are equal, but some are more equal than others'). All have a claim, though there may be functional differences, and in this context even differences in ministry between the general commitment of all believers to the community and specific services performed by the ministry, above all those of the leader (or the leadership team) of the community.[33]

Thus according to the New Testament, Christian churches are apostolic. This includes the apostolic proclamation of Jesus' own message (the kingdom of God), from which the person of Jesus and therefore his death and resurrection cannot be detached: 'the gospel of Jesus, the Son of God' (Mark 1.1) or 'the gospel of God' (Mark 1.14). This apostolicity of the Christian community stands in a reciprocal relationship to the apostolicity of the ministry (the so-called 'apostolic succession'). The apostolicity of the Christian community always implies the apostolic communication of the faith and therefore also the permanent importance of the foundation document in which the 'gospel of Jesus' is related in kerygmatic form: the New Testament read against the horizon of understanding of what is called the 'Old Testament'. The apostolicity of the content of the faith of the community is decisive for the New Testament: 'What you have heard from me before many witnesses entrust to faithful men who will be able to teach others also' (II Tim. 2.2). The prime concern is with an unbroken succession or continuity, less in the ministry than in the apostolic tradition or content of faith.

The basic self-understanding of the Christian community follows from this: it is 'a community of God' by being a community of Jesus, i.e. by assembling as a community around Jesus as salvation from God, in accordance with the testimony of the apostles.

Simply from a sociological perspective, this community has

the right to leaders. For a community of God this right is also an apostolic right. Moreover, as a community of Christ it has an ecclesiological right, by grace, to celebrate the eucharist on the basis of Jesus' mandate, 'Do this in remembrance of me'. The New Testament communities and those of the early church lived on the basis of this apostolic orientation.

Only when the first generation, above all that of apostles and prophets, had disappeared, did all the churches of their own accord expressly tackle the problem of 'church leadership' (roughly between AD 80 and 100). This was a problem with which Paul himself was intensively preoccupied before his death, which he expected at that time (see Phil. 2.19–24). At the same time this is precisely the period in which the ministry did not just take on specific, albeit still very changeable contours in the different communities, but at the same time became the subject of theological reflection, although here there was less interest in specific structures of ministry and the names given to ministers.

Those who held office in the church in the post-apostolic period had to be concerned for the apostolic origin of their existence, i.e. the gospel, from which the communities needed to live; in other words, for their Christian identity and power to make men whole through the vitality of the gospel. Here ministry is embedded in the totality of all kinds of other services which are needed for building up the community, just as the dedication of the whole community is itself necessary for this building up (Eph. 4.11). The uniqueness and particular character of the charisma of the ministry within many other charismata and gifts lies in the fact that those who hold office, in solidarity with the whole of the community, nevertheless have their own unalienable responsibility for preserving the community in its apostolic identity and in the authentic gospel. In this connection the requirement of apostolicity, not the mode of appointment, was the theologically relevant factor for the New Testament. So the apostolicity of the communities founded through the 'apostles and prophets' is the basis and source of the apostolicity of the church's ministry as well.

(d) Some criteria of this apostolicity

1. 'Apostolic' first of all signifies the awareness of the community that it is carrying on the cause of Jesus. What is this cause? Jesus was the eschatological prophet of the kingdom of God, i.e. of God as salvation for mankind: of God's liberating

action. Where God 'reigns', communication prevails among
men and women and brotherhood develops. This is a proclamation which, moreover, can be seen and experienced in the
action of Jesus, in his life-style which is in conformity to the
demands of this kingdom. Thus the coming of the kingdom of
God as salvation for men and women is at the same time intrinsically bound up with the emergence of Jesus and his whole
person. In the New Testament this is all expressed in the technical term 'the gospel of Jesus as the Christ, Son of God'. Thus
in specific terms 'apostolic' already implies: the apostolic proclamation of Jesus' own message, from which the person of
Jesus, and therefore also his death and resurrection, may not
be separated. The apostolic interpretation of Jesus' rejection and
death is part of the heart of the gospel. Thus what we have
here is in the end 'the gospel of God' (Mark 1.14), first of all
because Jesus' message had as its content the coming rule of
God, but also because God also clearly has something to say to
us in and through the death of this 'divine messenger'. Jesus is
therefore an essential constituent of the gospel as 'the gospel of
God'.

2. The apostolic mediation of the faith of the Christian communities also has as a specific consequence the permanent importance of the foundation document in which the 'gospel of
Jesus as the Christ' is told in kerygmatic form: the New Testament interpreted against the background of what was called the
Old Testament. This is where the inspiration of the Christian
community lies: this book 'is inspired' because it inspires us,
just as God inspired Jesus and his movement. Thus the way in
which the community stands under the norm of the New Testament is also part of what I call the 'apostolicity' of the community (despite the necessary but precarious task of any biblical
hermeneutics).

3. The fundamental self-understanding of the Christian community becomes clear from this: it is a 'community of God'
through being a 'community of Jesus': the community stands
under the apostolic norm of 'discipleship of Jesus' which is to
be realized again and again in new historical circumstances.

4. Proclamation, liturgy and *diakonia* (i.e. concern for suffering humanity and human society) are apostolic characteristics
of the communities of God.

5. This community has an apostolic right to a minister or
ministers, and also a right, on the basis of the New Testament
mandate, 'Do this in remembrance of me', to the celebration of
the eucharist or the Lord's Supper.

6. From an apostolic perspective the communities are clearly not isolated entities but bound together in love (although in New Testament times there was not as yet an organization which extends beyond a particular region); a great *koinonia* or brotherly community in which mutual criticism, grounded in the gospel, must be possible if all communities are to be maintained on apostolic lines. For the New Testament, this bond of love seems to be maintained in its apostolicity by the collegial leadership and *koinonia* of all ministers, in which the function of Peter is a binding unitive factor in maintaining the bond of love.

7. Ministry in the church is not a status or state but a service, a function within the 'community of God' and therefore a 'gift of the Holy Spirit'. Suffering solidarity with the poor and insignificant is an essential mark of the apostolicity of the ministry, since it is an apostolic mark of the whole community of Jesus.

8. Finally, the specific, legitimate contemporary forms of the apostolicity of the community and therefore of the ministry (which are constantly changing) cannot be discovered in purely theoretical terms, but only in a mutually critical correlation (which must be both theoretical and practical) between what the New Testament churches did and what the Christian communities do now.

This survey shows that as far as the New Testament is concerned the community has a right to a minister or ministers and to the celebration of the eucharist. This apostolic right has priority over the criteria for admission which the church can and may impose on its ministers (see already I Tim. 3.1–13). Of course some criteria are attached to the purpose and content of the ministry in the service of a community of God. However, the apostolic right of Christian communities may not be made null and void by the official church; this is itself bound by this apostolic right. Therefore if in changed circumstances there is a threat that a community may be without a minister or ministers (without priests), and if this situation becomes increasingly widespread, then criteria for admission which are not intrinsically necessary to the nature of the ministry and are also in fact a cause of the shortage of priests, must give way to the original, New Testament right of the community to leaders. In that case this apostolic right has priority over the church order which has in fact grown up and which in other circumstances may have been useful and healthy (this is a point to which I shall return in detail later).

II

Ministry in the First and Second Christian Millennia

A. A pneumatological and ecclesial conception of the ministry in the first ten centuries

1. The evidence of the Council of Chalcedon

If we are to put the ministry of the church as it was practised in the first ten centuries into clear focus, we would do well to begin with canon 6 of the Council of Chalcedon (451). This canon represents very well in legalistic form the view and practice of the early church in connection with the ministry. Patristic theology and the liturgies of the early church are a clear confirmation of this Chalcedonian conception of the ministry, which in the last resort seeks to canalize a loose form of practising the ministry which had earlier still been in process of change.

The canon does not condemn just any form of 'absolute consecration', in other words, a 'consecration' of a candidate without any connection with a particular community, but declares this to be invalid: 'No one may be "ordained" priest or deacon in an absolute manner (*apolelymenōs*) . . . unless a local community is clearly assigned to him, whether in the city or in the country, whether in a martyrdom (burial place where a martyr was venerated) or in a monastery'; then 'the holy council resolves that their *cheirotonia* (*ordinatio* or appointment) is null and void . . . and that they may not therefore perform functions on any occasion'.[1] This text displays a clearly defined view of ministry in the church. Only someone who has been called by a particular community (the people and its leaders) to be its pastor and leader authentically receives *ordinatio* (I am deliberately not translating this term by 'consecration'). *Ordinatio* is an appointment or 'incorporation' as minister to a community which calls a particular fellow-Christian and indicates him as its leader (or, above all in the earlier period, which accepts the actual charismatic emergence of one of its members and gives it official confirmation). An 'absolute *ordinatio*', i.e. one in which hands are laid on someone without his being asked by a particular community to be its leader, is null and void. Here we can see an essentially ecclesial view of the ministry.

In the Roman empire, *ordinatio* means entry into a particular *ordo*; it was the classical expression for the naming of imperial functionaries, above all the king or emperor himself.[2] Tertullian was the first to use the word in a Christian sense, in connection with the ministry of the church: *ordo* is a list of successive bishops (one might say, a list of succession). Cyprian systematized this concept. *Ordinatio* then means (*a*) the canonical appointment of a Christian to the college of office-bearers, (*b*) as grace from God – the two key concepts of the New Testament.

In the Roman empire, *ordo* also had the connotation of particular social classes differing in status. The senators formed the 'higher order', into which one would be 'instituted' (*in-ordinari* or *ordinari*). Under the Gracchi, an order of *equites* came into being between the *ordo senatorum* and the *plebs*, or the people (here *ordinari* then means becoming an *eques*); only later was the *plebs* itself also called an *ordo*. Thus finally people talked of *ordo et plebs*, i.e. the upper, leading class, and the ordinary people, a terminology which not only introduced influence from the Old Testament but also coloured the difference between clergy and people (laity): after the time of Constantine the church *ordinatio* or appointment to the 'order of office-bearers' clearly became more attractive because the clergy were seen as a more exalted class in the church in comparison with the more lowly 'believers'.[3] The clericalization of the ministry had begun!

As such, then, the old church usage of *ordinatio* or *cheirotonoia* has nothing to do with the laying on of hands or *cheirothesia*, although the sending or calling of the church, and therefore the appointment of a Christian to the ranks of those holding office in the church, was in fact made by the laying on of hands (see further below). Therefore the essence, and indeed the force of the old concept of *ordinatio* comprises the calling, the mandate of the sending of someone by a particular Christian community (the people and its leaders). This is the essence of *ordinatio*, although (with a very few exceptions) in fact for several centuries, beginning even in the New Testament, this appointment was in fact made specifically by the bishop laying on hands with *epiclesis* or the prayer of the whole community. According to the canon of Chalcedon, even a correct liturgy of the laying

on of hands is null and void without calling by a local church
and to a local church. It is this particular context which determines the essentially ecclesial character of the ministry; the
ecclesial dimension is the decisive element of *ordinatio* or
appointment.

The community knows that it has the right, by grace, to
leaders; consequently, always along with the leaders it has already been given, it takes the initiative here. Moreover, in the
early church each local church is aware that it has everything
necessary for building up the real life of a 'community of Christ'
(at that time there were still no reservations from above). The
local church calls its own ministers. The essential connection
between community and ministry, expressed at the Council of
Chalcedon in canonical form, shows that the difference between
the power of ordination and the power of jurisdiction was not
only unknown at that time, but even inconceivable in ecclesiological terms.[4] Ministry is a concern of the local community.
Cyprian demands this right as being of divine origin, i.e. as
belonging to the nature of a 'community of God', even against
Pope Stephen.[5] 'No bishop is to be imposed on the people
whom they do not want.'[6] Leo the Great also puts the matter
succinctly: 'He who must preside over all must be chosen by
all.'[7] At the same time this all implies that the ministry is a
public matter and that therefore no one can appropriate the
ministry of his own accord. The mutual relationship between
community and ministry also points in this direction. The ministry is defined essentially in ecclesial terms, and not as an
ontological qualification of the person of the minister, apart
from the determinative context of the church. The story of Paulinus of Nola is characteristic here. He says that he was in fact
ordained in absolute form in Barcelona; he writes about this in
an ironically pious way, to this effect: 'There was I, orphaned,
shamefaced, priest, as it were, only to our dear Lord, but without a community: *in sacerdotium tantum Domini, non etiam in
locum Ecclesiae dedicatus.*'[8] Later, Isidore of Seville calls those
who are ordained absolutely, men without heads: 'neither man
nor beast'.[9] We know from the outsider Jerome that he reluctantly bowed to the pressure on him to be ordained presbyter,
on condition that he did not have to perform any ministerial
functions![10] Neither flesh nor fish, said the early church.

The canon of Chalcedon was known not only in the East but
also in the West, and here too it was valid for church lawyers
and theologians until the twelfth century. Pope Leo, lawyers
like Burchard of Worms, Ivo of Chartres, the *Decretum Gratiani*,

and various western synods and theologians down to the twelfth century, refer to the declaration of the invalidity of absolute ordinations made at Chalcedon.[11]

However, in the ancient church the link between the community and its leader was so strong that to begin with it was impossible for the leader to be moved to another community – although exceptions to the rule were made, justified by the principle of *oikonomia*,[12] i.e. on compassionate grounds. Another fundamental consequence of the canon of Chalcedon was that a minister who for any personal reason ceased to be the president of a community *ipso facto* returned to being a layman in the full sense of the word.[13] The distinction between jurisdiction, i.e. specific charge over a community, and *ordo*, the power of ordination in itself, did not exist at that time. So at that time the departure of a minister had quite a different significance from the present-day laicization of a priest. In other words, according to this view it is not the case that someone who has the power bestowed by ordination may preside over the community and therefore also at the community's eucharist. The minister appointed by the community already receives, by virtue of his appointment, all the powers which are necessary for the leadership of a Christian community; he receives them from the Holy Spirit via the community. This is because, since the community understood itself as the community of God – the temple of the Holy Spirit – people began to give this appointment of a minister a liturgical framework of its own in which God's charisma was called down on him. There was as yet nothing 'sacral' here because this was a sacramentalism of faith! This means that the modern situation in which a community might not be able to celebrate the eucharist because no priest is present is theologically inconceivable in the early church; the community chooses a president for itself and has hands laid on him so that they can also be a community which celebrates the eucharist, i.e. a 'community of God'. In that case the vitality of the community in terms of the gospel is the deciding factor, not the availability of a body of priestly manpower, crammed full of education in one place or another.

2. The evidence of the liturgy

This view of the ministry held by the early church, officially documented in canon 6 of Chalcedon, is also expressed in the earliest liturgy for the laying on of hands known to us, from the first half of the third century, the *Apostolic Tradition* of Hippolytus (and in the whole of the liturgical tradition which is influenced by it, above all the *Apostolic Constitutions* and the *Testamentum Domini*). It can also be found in the writings of the theologians of this time.[14] In the liturgical tradition,[15] the *ordinatio* (i.e. *cheirotonia* or appointment') of a bishop, presbyter or deacon comprises a variety of aspects.

First of all the institution of a bishop in a local church community:[16]

1. All the local community with its clergy chooses its own bishop, and the person who is called must in principle accept the choice of his own free will. We know from other documents that the one who was called was really expected to obey this call from the community, even against his own will. This happened, for example, to Ambrose and Augustine.[17] At all events, ministry is a necessary function for the community and therefore the community has the right to ministers. Furthermore, the local church tests the apostolic faith of the candidate and bears witness to it.[18] This is an expression of the ancient conviction that primarily the community itself is apostolic; but because in turn the bishop takes on a specific responsibility for the community and thus for its apostolicity,[19] the community which receives him first examines the apostolic foundation of his faith.

2. Episcopal laying on of hands with *epiclesis*, or the prayer of the whole community to the Spirit: Although the local church chooses an episcopal minister of its own, it does not autonomously provide itself with a minister. Because he has been chosen by a 'community of Christ', his choice is experienced as a gift of the Holy Spirit. In the early church, as in the New Testament, the minister, the new bishop, was seen as a gift of the Spirit of Jesus. This was expressed sacramentally in the liturgy by the laying on of hands by bishops (later, according to the Council of Nicaea, at least three bishops), from neighbouring churches. This is an expression of the communion of all the Christian communities with one another. No local church has the monopoly of the gospel or of the apostolicity which derives from the gospel; it, too, is subject to criticism from the other apostolic churches. The presence of the leaders of other churches in the liturgy is primarily a witness which confirms the identity of the faith of this community with that of the others. There is therefore no local introversion; in this way there is a creative expression of the collegiality among the local churches. The (three) bishops lay their hands on the candidate, silently assisted by the whole of the council of presbyters, while the whole congregation prays in silence to God (as the president

asks out loud), for the power of the *pneuma hēgemonikon* and the *pneuma archieratikon*: the power of the spirit of leadership as pastor and leader, and the spirit of high priesthood. Before this it is said that God 'gave leaders (*archontes*) and priests (*hiereis*) to the generation of the righteous, the descendants of Abraham, i.e. the church': Moses and Aaron (in the Old Testament, the embodiments of theocratic secular and religious authority, Ezra 8.69; Neh. 12.12; Jer. 10.3; 31.7; Amos 1.15). It is said of the 'spiritual power of leadership' that God gave it to his Son (at his baptism in the Jordan), while he in turn gave it to the apostles, the founders of the churches, as a gift at Pentecost. Now this same 'spirit of leadership' (*spiritus principalis*, according to the Vulgate translation of Ps. 50.14), is called down upon the new candidate. In the strength of this charisma of leadership he will 'feed the flock' (a messianic term: Isa. 40.11; see Acts 20.28; I Peter 5.2). The minister (bishop) receives the prophetic mission to proclaim 'the word of grace' (a reference to Luke 4.22; Acts 14.3; 20.32), i.e. the good news of Jesus, which has been handed down by the apostles. In addition, 'the power of the high priestly charisma of the spirit' (*to pneuma to archieratikon; spiritum primatus sacerdotii*) is called down upon the candidate. God also gave this charisma of the Spirit to his Son, who gave it to the apostles: now the community asks God to pour out the same spirit of priesthood upon the new candidate. As the priestly leader of the community, the minister must (*a*) constantly speak for his community to the best of his ability before God (cf. Heb. 7.25; 9.24), above all asking for the forgiveness of sin; (*b*) the episcopal leader must also be a *sacerdos* in the sense of being president at the eucharist (*propherein ta dora*); (*c*) in the strength of the priestly charisma of the spirit he has authority to forgive sins (cf. Matt. 9.6; John 20.23); (*d*) he apportions and co-ordinates the *kleroi* (i.e. the duties of the ministers; specifically those of the presbyterate and diaconate); (*e*) he exercises the power to bind and to loose (see Matt. 18.18: impose a ban or lift a ban). He is to do all this 'humbly and with a pure heart' (see Matt. 5.5, 8; II Tim. 2.25). As earlier, in I Clement 42.1–4, here in the *Apostolic Tradition* there is a clear emphasis on one and the same power of the Spirit which goes from the Father to the Son, from the Son to the apostles, and which within the community built up on the apostles, together with its leaders, is now called down upon the one whom the community has chosen here and now to be its leader. The *ordinatio* is liturgically a matter of course because church leadership was experienced as a gift of the Spirit: participation in the prophetic and priestly[20] spiritual charisma of Jesus himself.

The *ordinatio* of a *presbyter*[21] was performed through the laying on of hands by the bishop, but in this case fellow presbyters also lay their hands on the candidate who has been put forward by the community. The variation in the spiritual charisma is clear from the *epiclesis*: '. . . give him the spirit of grace and counsel of the college of presbyters, so that he can help your people and lead them with a pure heart'.[22] Presbyters are compared with 'the elders whom Moses had chosen' (Num. 11.17–25). In the pre-Nicene church, presbyters as such might not preside at the eucharist; therefore nothing is said about a charisma for this in the liturgical *ordinatio* according to the *Traditio* of Hippolytus. However, with the bishop's permission the presbyter might also replace the *sacerdos*, i.e. the bishop, here (without a supplementary 'ordination' being thought necessary). At that time there were still no 'parishes'; there were only dioceses consisting of towns. As the church spread, in smaller communities presbyters in fact took over the episcopal 'leadership and priesthood' within their communities. From that stage on – differing from one area to another – presbyters too gradually come to be called *sacerdotes*.[23] As a result, sacramentally, the difference between bishop and priest really became problematical; a pastor is in fact as it were bishop of a parish, just as many bishops in Italy now do what in Holland is assigned to a rural dean. Such historical differences demonstrate that the direct relationship to the community determines the concept *sacerdos*.

The *ordinatio* of a chosen *deacon* was performed in roughly the same way, with the difference that the college of presbyters was not involved, because at that time a deacon was exclusively at the disposal of the bishop and not of the presbyters. So he does not receive the spiritual charisma in which the council of presbyters shares because he is not a member of it.[24] His charisma remains 'open'; he receives his spiritual charisma 'on the authority of the bishop': thus he can and may do all that the bishop specifically requires him to do.

In these three instances of *ordinatio* Hippolytus does not set out to prescribe invariable formulae. Rather, his *Traditio* is meant as an aid towards the improvisation of presidents: 'provided that the prayer be orthodox.' [25] At that time no liturgical appointment or *ordinatio* was necessary for other church ministries, e.g. those of lectors and subdeacons.[26]

This evidence from the *Apostolic Tradition* and the *Apostolic Constitutions* is also important because it is a recognizable parallel to the later canon 6 of Chalcedon. As in Chalcedon, there is a clear expression of the ecclesial and pneumatological conception of the ministry in the early church: ministry comes from below, but this is experienced as a 'gift of the Spirit' and therefore 'from above'. The charismata imparted derive from the fullness of the Spirit with which Jesus himself was filled and with which he fills the church. After Vatican II, in 1969, this tradition from Hippolytus was taken up in the new *Pontificale Romanum*, which explicitly seeks once again to bring present-day tradition into line with the early church – by no means a small achievement (above all thanks to B. Botte, who edited the Hippolytus text).

In this liturgy the decisive element is the gift of the power of the Spirit (no distinction is made between 'grace' and 'character': in this respect it is a charisma of the Spirit.) This is further underlined by what the *Traditio* says about the *confessores-martyres*, Christians who have been arrested and have suffered for the cause of Christ, but who for fortuitous reasons have not been put to death. Because of their suffering as a witness to the faith, any person of this kind has the charisma of the Spirit. Whenever a community subsequently chooses him as a minister (deacon or priest, at any rate), no hands need to be laid upon him (this is, however, necessary if he is to be made a bishop).[27] He already has the necessary power of the Spirit. It is important that for these candidates, too, there was nevertheless a liturgical appointment to a particular community (leaving out the laying on of hands). Here we can clearly see the twofold dimension of the old *ordinatio*: on the one hand appointment by the church (its ecclesial aspect in the context of church order) and on the other hand the charisma of the Spirit (the pneumatological and christological aspect). It must be said that what was later called the power of ordination and its character is simply the appointment of a minister to a particular community along with the gift of the Spirit (whether institutional, or spontaneous and charismatic), differentiated in accordance with different ministerial duties. The recognition of someone as a minister by the church (people and leaders) is decisive.

Thus the actual structures of official ministry in the ancient church consisted of leaders within a specialized team. In addition to this, of course, there are all kinds of other ministries in the church, like those of 'teachers' and lectors, but according to the *Traditio* of Hippolytus these need no liturgical or ecclesial appointment. Such people have adequate spiritual resources for these tasks as a result of their membership of the priestly people of God.[28] Of course questions of prestige also played a role in the church's ministry (above all between presbyters and deacons); in the last resort, however, given the main outlines of everyone's task, the boundaries are nevertheless very fluid. The chief difference from the New Testament is that in principle the tasks which in the New Testament period were differentiated are now brought together in one ministry, that of the bishop. Later this would lead some theologians to the theory that there is really only one ministry, i.e. that of the bishop, and all other ministries are only participating functions of this. This seems to me to be a possible and legitimate theological interpretation, but not a necessary one. I disagree with Karl Rahner, who has been foremost in proposing it as the only possible theory; it seems to me to be a speculative possibility rather than to have a historical foundation in the facts presented by the New Testament. For all its pluriformity the ministry in the church is essentially collegiality, i.e. solidarity of Christians equipped with different charismata of ministry.

3. Appointment to an order and the liturgical framework of the laying on of hands

Because of its complicated history, I feel that I should give a further analysis of the relationship between *ordinatio* and the specific laying on of hands (with *epiclesis*).

In the Latin church, the term 'laying on of hands' (*impositio manuum*) renders both the Greek *cheirotonia* and *cheirothesia*. *Cheirotonia* really means 'appointment' (signifying with the hand); *cheirothesia*, however, means laying on of hands. Now in the texts of the Eastern churches, above all before the eighth century, *cheirotonia* and *cheirothesia* are used interchangeably without any deliberate theological difference.[29] Only after the Second Council of Nicaea (787) does the difference between the two terms become sharper, and from the twelfth century onwards in the Eastern churches *cheirothesia* is used exclusively for the institution or *ordinatio* of bishops, presbyters and deacons, whereas *cheirotonia* is reserved for appointment to other church ministries. Even then, however no special theological value seems to be attached to this distinction.

In the Western church, as well as *ordinatio* we find simply the term *impositio manuum* as a translation of both *cheirotonia* and *cheirothesia*. It appears from Jerome[30] that the bishops are always chosen from the college of presbyters, without a new laying on of hands being given; the choice of the bishop by the presbyteral college (always with the approval of the people) was enough (the analogy with the choice of a Roman consul is striking), although this was in no way a general custom. On the other hand, in the earliest Latin ritual of consecration (*Ordo 34*, Andrieu), from the eighth century, at the *ordinatio* of ministers of the church there is no mention of a laying on of hands, though Andrieu (in contrast to C. Vogel) presupposes this. At the beginning of the fifteenth century Macarius of Ancyra can still write that the choice of a community makes someone a bishop; here the laying on of hands is secondary.[31] Thus although the laying on of hands at *ordinatio* is a clear fact of the tradition, it is not regarded as the most important thing; what is essential is the church's mandate or the church's sending of the minister, not the specific form in which the calling and sending takes shape. For this reason, too, the liturgical laying on of hands at the *ordinatio* of ministers does not have any effect in heterodox churches. In the first millennium, both in the East and in the West, the necessity for the laying on of hands at the *ordinatio* of ministers was strongly relativized:[32] recognition and sending by the church is the really decisive element. This sending is essentially an act of the sacramental church; because it is self-evident it is therefore also given specific form in a particular liturgical act consisting in the laying on of hands. The history of the first millennium therefore leaves completely open the question whether the rite of consecration is absolutely necessary. Above all, the Eastern practice of the *oikonomia* in connection with the laying on of hands in heterodox churches is a clear indication that the all-decisive element is not the liturgical rite as such, but the sending by the church, though in practice (with one or two exceptions), the sending was always carried out in and through the specific liturgy of the laying on of hands.

Thus it emerges from an analysis of *ordinatio*, *cheirotonia* and *cheirothesia* that the basic principle is that the minister of the church is one who is recognized as such by the whole of the church community (the people and its leaders), and is sent out to a particular community. As Pope Leo I put it: if the candidate is chosen by the clergy and wanted by the people;[33] in Leo's time this recognition, which was essential, was implemented by the laying on of hands by the candidate's own bishop with the assent of the metropolitan (loc. cit.). Outside this ecclesial context the liturgical laying on of hands is voided of all meaning. In the twelfth and thirteenth centuries a new theology of the ministry, moving in another direction, would alter the perspective completely, at least in the West.

We can again conclude: the essential nucleus of *ordinatio* is being recognized as a minister through the church and in this way being chosen for a particular church community (through its leaders with the explicit approval of the believing community, or *vice versa*). Normally this is given specific form in a liturgical laying on of hands, but that is not primary or all decisive.

4. The first 'sacerdotalizing' of the church's ministry

(a) Sacerdos *(bishop; priest) and eucharist*

It emerges above all from the pre-Nicene literature that the ancient church had difficulty in calling the church leaders 'priestly'. According to the New Testament, Christ and the Christian community alone were priestly; the leaders were at the service of Christ and the priestly people of God, but are themselves never said to be priestly. However, Cyprian was one of the first to have a clear predilection for the Old Testament priestly sacrificial terminology, to which he compared the Christian eucharist. In this way the sacerdotalizing of the vocabulary of the church's ministry in fact developed gradually,[34] though this was at first in an allegorical sense. Furthermore, Cyprian is also the first who says of the *sacerdos*, i.e. at that time the bishop who presides over the community and therefore at the eucharist, that he does this *vice Christi*, in Jesus' place.[35] By contrast, Augustine continues to refuse to call bishops and presbyters priests in the real sense, in the sense of being mediators between Christ and the community.[36] In his *Traditio*, Hippolytus is in a transitional period. In his *epiclesis* there is outright mention of 'the Spirit of high priesthood' which falls to the part of the bishop who presides, but on the other hand Hippolytus repeatedly says that the bishop is like a high priest (*Traditio* 3 and 34); the Old Testament allegorical usage is still played on. However, these comparisons are not made in the case of presbyters, who thus are clearly non-priestly (not a *sacerdos* or leader), although as time goes on (varying according to different local communities) they increasingly replace the bishop as presidents at the eucharist (without needing a new 'consecration' for this). In the pre-Nicene period it is therefore hard to speak of priests in connection with both bishops and presbyters. For the early church *sacerdos* (as an Old Testament name for the Jewish priest) was applied allegorically, and to begin with only to the bishop,[37] who was then the figure with whom the local community really identified and in whom it found its unity. Because in the long run presbyters also normally presided at the eucharist (because they in fact were the local leaders of smaller communities), they too were finally called priests (*sacerdotes*), albeit *secundi meriti*, i.e. subordinate to the episcopal president.[38] Thus a first sacerdotalizing, at least of the vocabulary connected with ministers, came into being.

The development which I have just outlined seems to suggest a link in the early church between 'priesthood' and the eucharist. However, this is not the case, or at least it is not the whole truth. In the early church there was really an essential link between the community and its leader, and therefore between the community leader and the community celebrating the eucharist. This nuance is important. It was essentially a matter of who presided over the community (as an individual or in a team): 'We do not receive the sacrament of the eucharist. . .from anyone other than the president of the community', says Tertullian.[39] In fact at that time the bishop was the real leader of the community. In that case no eucharist could be celebrated against the will of the bishop.[40] The purpose of this rule (for both 'Ignatius' and Cyprian) was that of preserving the unity of the community. The figure who gives unity to the community also presides in 'the sacrament of church unity',[41] the eucharist. Although the problem of the ministry is involved here, the prime factor is the apostolicity and the unity of the church: 'outside the church community there is no eucharist'.[42] In the first instance this means that a 'heretical community' has no right to the eucharist; the question of the ministry in connection with the president at the eucharist is subordinate to this.[43]

Furthermore, in the ancient church the whole of the believing community concelebrated, albeit under the leadership of the one who presided over the community. A later, but still early *Liber Pontificalis* writes: *tota aetas concelebrat*,[44] the whole of the community, young and old, concelebrates. Some readers may already be asking whether 'concelebrate' then had the precise meaning which it has acquired now that it has become a twentieth-century technical term. The critical question to ask in reply is, on what grounds can one give a kind of theological priority to a narrowed-down technical meaning? This can just as much be a narrowing of perspective. In the early church, presiding at the eucharist was simply the liturgical dimension of the many-sided ministerial pattern of presiding in the Christian community. The one who is recognized by the church as leader of the community also presides at the eucharist.

Of course, for the early church the community itself is the active subject of the *offerimus panem et calicem*.[45] We may not define the specific function of the *sacerdos* who presides at the eucharist in terms of the later interpolations into liturgical books (such as e.g. *accipe potestatem offerre sacrificium* and *sacerdos oportet offerre*, which already presupposes a later *potestas sacra* in the priest, isolated from the church community and thus absolute). In the solemn *eucharistia* (which to begin with, of course, was improvised), the prayer of praise and thanksgiving, or *anaphora*, spoken by the president, he speaks primarily as the prophetic leader of the community with pastoral responsibility, who proclaims the history of salvation, and therefore praises, lauds and thanks God, and thus proclaims the presence of salvation for the assembled community in the eucharist. The active subject of the eucharist was the community. It was for this reason that the president accepted the offertory from the whole of the community, gifts which through the spirit were transformed into the gift of Jesus' body and blood. Y. Congar, D. Droste, R. Schultze, K. J. Becker, R. Berger and many others have shown quite clearly how in the early church the *ecclesia* itself is the integral subject of liturgical, including eucharistic, action. The 'I' of the president never solely, or predominantly, indicated the subject of the celebrant of the eucharist.[46] So at that time concelebration was not limited to a common celebration of the eucharist by concelebrating priests, but was the term for the concelebration of the whole of the believing people who were present.[47] The people celebrates, and the priest presides simply as the servant of all. Even where the reference is expressly made to concelebrating priests, there was only one president; the others concelebrate 'silently'. There is no question of a *recitatio communis* of the canon (said to be necessary for a valid 'concelebration') in the early church.[48] So in the early church the eucharist could always take place when the community met together.

(b) Could a layman preside at the eucharist?

The question whether a layman could preside at the eucharist is a modern one. The early church would have found it perverse. First of all, we see that in the early church the bishop, who at that time was the real leader of the community, albeit in a collegial association with his presbyters, presided by himself at the eucharist, even at a concelebration. He was the figure symbolizing the unity of the church. Gradually (with the growth of communities – originally cities – into what we should now call church provinces) his presbyteral helpers or presbyters received permission to preside at the eucharist in his absence (although at that time they were in no way consecrated for this) because in such a situation they are in fact the actual community leaders (*sacerdotes*). I Clement already assumes that it is normal for the *episkopos* presbyter to preside at the eucharist, but he adds: 'or other eminent members, with the approval of the whole church', since 'everything must be done in order'.[49] Thus the decisive element is the acceptance of a president by the church. Ignatius, who calls the bishop, as the figure with whom the community identifies, the real president in the eucharist, also recognizes instances in which he can and may be replaced.[50] Here he does not once explicitly name presbyters or deacons as potential substitutes.

Nevertheless, in the early church we have only one explicit piece of evidence that if need be a layman, too, could preside at the eucharist. Tertullian, who nevertheless makes a sharp distinction between *ordo* (appointment to the ministry) and *plebs*, the believing people or the laity, writes that in normal circumstances, presiding at the eucharist is by definition a role for the leader of the community; for him this is specifically the bishop with his council of presbyters. However, he says, 'But where no college of ministers has been appointed, you, the laity, must celebrate the eucharist and baptize; in that case you are your own priests, for where two or three are gathered together, there is the church, even if these three are lay people.'[51] The fact that the church community is itself a priestly people of God had a fundamental significance, above all in the pre-Nicene church, although the name 'priest' was not applied to individual Christians but to the Christian community as a collective whole.[52] On this basis, in exceptional circumstances the community itself chose its president *ad hoc*. Although Augustine was opposed to the sacerdotalizing of the ministers of the church, in the sense that bishop or presbyter might become mediators between God and the people, in contrast he explicitly denied the 'laity' any right to preside at the eucharist even in situations of emergency.[53] Nevertheless, what Tertullian says is in no way inspired by the Montanists; he accuses the Montanists precisely of allowing laity to celebrate at the eucharist without there being extreme need, and says that in so doing they deny the specific character of the ministry.[54] Tertullian's vision is not so isolated in the early church as one might think, though the imprecise terminology clearly plays a part here. Anyone who in such circumstances was required by the community to pre-side over the community (and thus at the eucharist) *ipso facto* became a minister by the acceptance of the church: he was instituted, i.e. became the authorized leader of the community. That is precisely what Augustine had in mind, so that despite the terminological difference there was a real consensus here. The specific character of the ministry was defended by all, but not a sacral power of consecration or a specific way in which institution to the ministry takes place.

In contrast to these conceptions of the ministry, in the second millennium a primarily juridical view of the ministry comes into being, almost exclusively concentrated on the ministry and less concentrated on the church, in which 'sacrament' and 'law' are detached from each other.

B. *The Second Christian Millennium: the notion of the church fades into the background and privatization begins*

1. The great change in the twelfth and thirteenth centuries: the mediaeval image of the priest

(a) *The shift in the significance of the canon of Chalcedon:* 'titulus ecclesiae'

A quite fundamental change in attitude from this view of the ministry in the early church was sanctioned in principle by two Ecumenical Councils – though after the Photian schism they were in fact predominantly Latin: the Third and Fourth Lateran Councils, in 1179 and 1215 respectively. In different respects both councils mark the beginning of a new practice in the church (following the introduction of the law of abstinence at the end of the fourth century and the clericalization after the time of Constantine, there were distant forerunners to this new practice in the first millennium).

Even in the Middle Ages, the *Decretum Gratiani* had again pointed to canon 6 of Chalcedon, which prohibits 'absolute ordinations',[55] and in a theological context, in the twelfth century, Hugo of Saint Victor, among others, had already referred to this canon. However, the Third Lateran Council broke with the Chalcedonian view, in practice if not in principle. The *titulus ecclesiae*, on the basis of which men were ordained, according to Chalcedon, was radically reinterpreted in 1179. Formerly men could only be ordained if they had been put forward by a particular community as minister (an essential element of the *ordinatio* or appointment), so that 'absolute ordinations' were invalid. Under Pope Alexander III the ecclesiological *titulus ecclesiae* was interpreted feudally to mean: no one may be ordained 'unless he has been assured of a proper living'.[56] Here, at least in principle, the old ecclesial practice is not denied, but it is predominantly seen (given the troubled feudal period) from the perspective of the financial support of the priest. I infer that this was in no way meant to be a break with the past from the fact that in 1189, ten years after this council, Pope Innocent (once again, but for the last time in church history) recalls the invalidity of absolute ordinations. However, he adds that on compassionate grounds and in accordance with an old custom of *oikonomia*, priests who have been ordained in a absolute manner may exercise priestly functions on condition that the bishop who ordains them provides for their support.[57]

Given the economic and social conditions of those days, with their many vagrant priests, the provision of support for clergy was certainly an acute question, which needed to be controlled. This does not do away with the fact that in current interpretation the old *titulus ecclesiae* was in fact reduced to the purely feudal question of a *beneficium*. The early Christian undercurrent was not denied, but in developing scholastic theology it was the surface current which came into its own, and did so, some centuries later, at the Council of Trent.[58] One has or feels a priestly calling; one makes it known (the link with the local church is not completely lost), is then trained as a priest and finally ordained. The implications are clear: the ordained man simply waits for the place to which his bishop will appoint him as priest! *Ordinatio* remains, in the abstract, the appointment of a Christian as minister in a diocesan area, though his specific placing is still left open. Here the claim of the community, which was originally an essential element of *ordinatio*, disappears. I am not in any way arguing that in Christendom, as the Middle Ages were called, this new usage can directly be identified with the 'absolute ordinations' which Chalcedon declared to be invalid. In new circumstances, literal repetition of the past still does not necessarily represent faithfulness to the great tradition. In my view the new practice does not in any way need to be called 'absolute ordination', though since then there have certainly been many invalid absolute ordinations, above all of monks who simply began to say private masses. Here I am thinking of the pious irony of Paulinus of Nola: I am a priest *in sacerdotium tantum Domini*, and not as pastor or leader in a community.

The Third Lateran Council already distinguishes the second Christian millennium sharply from the first; however, this shift is emphasized even further by the Fourth Lateran Council, and specifically by its declaration that the eucharist can be celebrated only 'by a priest who has been validly and legitimately ordained'.[59] This need not in itself come into conflict with practice in the first millennium, but it is a much narrower version of that practice: the link with choice by the community, the ecclesial nature of the ministry, threatens to disappear. Furthermore, the ecclesial dimension of the eucharist is reduced to the 'celebrating priest'. The history leading up to the two councils and above all their effect will show the full consequences of this narrowing of the church's view. The really fundamental change evidently came about not so much on the basis of theological criteria but above all for non-theological reasons. Similarly, the effect of the councils was not the result of theological intuitions but rather of non-theological presuppositions. And this fact in itself is a good enough reason why the earlier ecclesial view of the ministry should have priority over the conception which has been regarded as official since then.

(b) Causes of this new image of the priest

Indeed it might well be asked how this fundamental change in the church's view of its ministers could have taken place historically. Some historians and other writers put the whole of the blame on the fact that precisely at the time of the Third and Fourth Lateran Councils, the theory emerged of a mysterious sacramental character, the basis of the whole *sacramentum ordinis*.[60] I think that this is quite wrong, above all because the so-called major scholastic theologians, that is, Bonaventura, Albertus Magnus and Thomas Aquinas, interpreted the very vague theory of the character (which dated from the end of the twelfth century), however modern it then was, in continuity with the early church. Despite their diverging interpretations, for them character points to the visible link between 'ministry' and 'church'.[61] Furthermore, this character was given at all ordinations, from bishop to acolyte and sacristan. The term *mancipatio* – to be called to and accepted by the community for a particular service in the church – was the most tangible point of this character in the Middle Ages; and in essentials this followed the conception of the ministry in the early church.

Nevertheless, this scholastic doctrine contained elements which, much later, would contribute to an ontological and even magical sacerdotalizing of the priesthood. The germs of this are also present in the Middle Ages, but they were only projected on to the mediaeval theory of the character from later contexts. What are these other contextual factors?

From the sixth century on, the Popes had become the pawns of the emperors with their still influential Byzantine Caesaropapism. The spiritual renewal which the Irish missionaries brought to the continent of Europe had a completely different spirit from that to which 'Germanic' and 'Gallic' Christians had become accustomed. We can follow many historians in saying that with the conversion of the 'barbarians' the church was made barbarian! Bishops who formerly had been independent and free now became the servants of powerful seigneurs, secular lords, who to enhance their status built private churches and secured clergy for them at whim. The Carolingian renaissance indeed brought a reaction against this, but at the same time it consolidated the whole feudal system of foundations and donations. Even the Council of Aix-la-Chapelle (818–819), which wanted a spiritual renewal of the clergy,[62] primarily occupied itself with foundations (of churches) and donations, with an eye to the beginnings of feudalism, although an attempt was made to withdraw the nomination of priests from the meddling of secular seigneurs. As part of this feudal system, spiritual autonomy was restored to the bishops. Nevertheless, under the incipient feudal system, kings, counts and dukes had priests and even bishops under their control.

At that time, *ecclesia* was no longer a living community as before, but often simply a status symbol of secular rulers with 'private churches'. The involvement of the church in feudalism gave rise to prince bishops, who were hardly well versed in the great church tradition. It has to be acknowledged that in this confused situation the reform of Gregory VII was nothing short of a downright revolution. At the end of the eleventh century Gregory sought to extricate the church from its feudal entanglements. The Gregorian reform marked the beginning of a constantly recurring 'evangelical movement' – in spite of everything – which kept cropping up in the Middle Ages.

However, towards the end of the eleventh century and the beginning of the twelfth there was also a renaissance of Roman law. Its influence seems to me to have been decisive, above all in ecclesiology and therefore also in connection with the church's view of the ministry. This particular legal view, also through the feudal context, detached the power of leadership (in whatever sphere) from the concept of 'territoriality' and therefore, in the religious sphere, from the concept of the 'local church' – territoriality and local church must be seen above all as a 'human sphere' (not purely geographical). At the end of the thirteenth century this would lead to the famous remark of Vincent de Beauvais, *'quodque principi placuit, legis habet vigorem'*:[63] the principle of the 'fullness of power' (*plenitudo potestatis*); authority as value-in-itself apart from the community, in the civic and the ecclesiastical spheres.

Thus non-theological factors (feudal and legal) made the mediaeval 'theological' shift possible. Before that, for Christians the boundary between the 'spirit of Christ' and the 'spirit of the world' lay in their baptism: their sense of being accepted into the elect community of God's *ecclesia*; now, with the massive expansion of the church, this boundary came to lie above all at the point of the 'second baptism', that of monastic life. However, in the earliest period monks were laymen, not priests. The Christian community saw them as the deepest realization of their ideal Christian model. This perspective was shifted, to some degree through the Carolingian Council of Aix-la-Chapelle, but above all after the Gregorian reform. At a time when virtually everyone was baptized, the boundary between 'the spirit of Christ' and 'the spirit of the world' came to lie with the clergy. As a result the priesthood was seen more as 'a personal state of life', a *'status'*, than as a service to the community; it was personalized and privatized.[64] In particular the new conceptions of law, *ius*, and thus of jurisdiction, brought about a division between the power of ordination and the power of jurisdiction,[65] in my view one of the most fundamental factors which marks off the second Christian millennium from the first. At any rate, here lawyers developed the idea of 'sacred power' (*sacra potestas*), strongly influenced by the context in which they lived. *Potestas* is the stake in the whole of the investiture controversy between *imperium and sacerdotium*, emperor and pope, and the sphere of their authority. For the theology of the church, however, the division between the power of ordination and the power of jurisdiction meant the opening of the door to absolute ordinations. For although the ordained man might not be assigned a Christian community (i.e., legally speaking, had no *potestas iurisdictionis*), by virtue of *ordinatio* he had all priestly power in his own person. Only now did *ordinatio* in fact become a sacred rite (*weihe*): a man is a priest quite apart from a particular *ecclesia* (in other words, the definition of what Chalcedon had called an invalid 'absolute ordination'). This view opens up the way to practices which would have been unthinkable to earlier Christians, above all the private mass.[66] If a man has been personally ordained priest, he has the 'power of the eucharist' and can therefore celebrate it on his own. For the early church this was quite simply inconceivable.[67]

This was the origin of a theology of the ministry with another orientation. This is already evident from the new church documents, in which, in contrast to the first centuries, it is explicitly said that if the rite of the laying on of hands is performed in due order, albeit in the context of an 'absolute consecration', this consecration of the minister is valid and in force. This is connected with the developing conception of the *opus operatum* of the sacrament through which the ecclesial context is forced into the background. This is particularly evident in documents of Pope Innocent III (1198–1216). At that time in the West, after the revival of Roman law, the old principle of *oikonomia* was widely adapted to become the so-called principle of dispensation. Innocent III practised this principle in such sovereign fashion that in practice all absolute consecrations were valid.[68]

The consequence of all this is that the old relationship between *ministerium* and *ecclesia*, between ministry and church, now shifts to a relationship between *potestas* and *eucharistia*, the power of consecration and the eucharist. Moreover, this change is brought about in what is by no means a fortuitous semantic shift, i.e. the mediaeval semantic shift between *corpus verus Christi* and *corpus mysticum Christi*.[69] In the ancient church the theological and liturgical documents had constantly said that it is necessary to hold an ecclesial office to preside in the church, i.e. in the *corpus verum Christi*: leadership of the community. However, after the dispute over the eucharist between Rhatramnus and Lanfranc this terminology had begun to be confused. In the ancient church, *corpus mysticum Christi* did not mean the *ecclesia* but the eucharistic body of Christ. In the Middle Ages, however, things were different. Polemic altered the significance of the words. Thus whereas formerly it had been said that a minister needed to be ordained to preside over the church community (= *corpus verum*), the terminology now became that of presiding over the *corpus mysticum*, i.e. to celebrate the eucharist. The mediaeval *sacra potestas* which had grown up in the meantime began to influence this situation: ordination then became the bestowal of special power to be able to perform the consecration in the eucharist. As a logical consequence of this, the Fourth Lateran Council went on to say that only a validly ordained priest can speak the words of consecration. Thomas later produced a sharp formulation of what had developed since the twelfth century: 'Actions can be directed immediately to God in a twofold way. On the one hand, they can proceed from an individual person, like saying prayers, and so on; all those who are baptized are in a position to perform such an action. On the other hand, they can be performed by the whole church; and in this respect only the priest is capable of performing actions which are directed immediately to God, since the action of the whole church can be performed only by the person who consecrates the eucharist, which is the sacrament of the whole church.'[70] In comparison with the ancient church, circumstances here have taken a fundamentally different direction: a priest is ordained in order to be able to celebrate the eucharist; in the ancient church it is said that he is 'appointed' as minister in order to be able to appear as leader of the community; in other words, the community called him as leader to build up the community, and for this reason he was also the obvious person to preside at the eucharist. This shift is of the utmost importance: at all events, it is a narrower legalistic version of what the early church believed.

2. The 'modern view of the priest' after the fifteenth and sixteenth centuries

(a) Josse Clichtove (1472–1543)

Later, above all in the *ancien régime* of the absolute monarchy, these developments, which were partly also conditioned by feudalism, led to the image of the priest which was first formulated acutely by Josse Clichtove.[71] His view of the priest influenced the image of the priest at the Council of Trent (which for its part fought shy of Clichtove's exaggerations) and was developed further by Bérulle and Olier, through the Oratory and Saint-Sulpice, in other words throughout the so-called French school. It formed the background to all the spiritual literature about the priesthood in recent centuries down to Vatican II.

Clichtove combined biblical, patristic and mediaeval ideas with the situation of the modern society of his time. In itself this was a proper thing to do. However, in a hierarchical Christian society, governed by a power founded on divine law, the result was that by virtue of his state of life the priest is detached from the world, even from the world of the Christian laity. The idea of 'being taken out of the world', i.e. escape from the world, completely determines this image of the priest. The Levitical priestly laws from the Old Testament as well as the tradition of monastic life determined Clichtove's image of the priesthood. Priesthood is essentially defined by its relation with the cult (and not with the community). A priest, even a pastor, may have as little contact as possible even with his own parishioners, except for the necessary administration of the sacraments. To be a priest is to be a 'cultic priest'. Precisely on the basis of this relation to the cult, the priest is the one who is set apart from the people, and priestly celibacy is the only adequate expression of this essential separation. Therefore in his last works Clichtove even says that priestly celibacy goes back to the natural law and 'divine law', and that the legislation of the church alone can sanction this divine law. The consequence of this is that even the Pope cannot dispense with the law of celibacy. This is equivalent to the religious 'solemn vows' of an enclosed monk. Celibacy, regarded solely as restraint from what Clichtove calls fleshly impurity (*spurcitia*), is the *'claustrum'* that cuts off the priest from the world and segregates him. To give permission to the priest to marry would be equivalent to blurring the distinction between layman and priest. The whole of Clichtove's view is based on the supremely sacred power of the priest to offer sacrifice. Therefore 'religion' *par excellence* belongs to the caste of the priests and monks, who are far above the ordinary believers. Precisely on the basis of this power to offer sacrifice the priest is the mediator between God and believers.

Clichtove was concerned to work out a special 'priestly spirituality' for the large number of priests who had been consecrated at the beginning of the sixteenth century but had not been given any pastoral responsibility. In itself, this was a very dubious starting point, so that in addition, albeit for other reasons than for the religious life, he gives priestly spirituality more and more monastic features as time goes on. The basis of this 'modern spirituality of the priesthood' is the priestly 'state of grace'; this is essentially 'sacrificial' and is experienced in society in the priestly state; priesthood is less an office than a state, grounded in cultic activity. So it is understandable that Clichtove breaks with the conception of, for example, Thomas Aquinas, who sees the celibacy of the priesthood purely as a disciplinary measure of the church,[72] and makes a sharp distinction between the celibacy of the minister and the celibacy of religious and monks. For Clichtove, celibacy is an essential part of the cultic separation of the priest from the believing people. Only at this time does the image of the priest become completely clerical, hierarchical and monastic. The priest-theologian Clichtove wanted to present himself as the great, strict reformer of spirituality against the collapse of priestly morality in the late Middle Ages, against which both Luther and Erasmus had fulminated (he already did this before the break-through of the Reformation, which simply made him even more rigorous on some points). He wanted a new spirituality of the priesthood, but on the basis of a very narrow theological view of the church's ministry (which is not really a ministry but simply a state). Unfortunately he cast this already one-sided spirituality in juridical forms. Also, above all under his influence, the Catholic image of the priest came to be seen in the light of an absolutizing of the law, for which the mediaeval image of the priest had laid only a very few foundations. Furthermore, the image of the priest as the solitary private sayer of 'masses', without further pastoral responsibilities, took on a certain divine aura. The Council of Trent, faithful to its standpoint of not taking up any positions in theological controversies within Catholicism, refrained from sanctioning the basic views of Clichtove, although something of his spirit can already be felt in the actual canons of Trent.

(b) The Council of Trent on the church's ministry

It is no way my purpose to discuss the Tridentine doctrine of the 'sacrament of ordination',[73] except in connection with the differences in conceptions of the ministry between the first and second Christian millennia.

At the beginning of my account of the second millennium I already said that the church definitely did not intend a break with the church of the first millennium. On the contrary. They were convinced, rather, that they remained in line with the ancient church despite actual fundamental divergences caused by new situations in the church and the world. Both the continuity and the break clearly come to the fore in the Acts, and somewhat less in the final reaction of the canons of the Council of Trent.

The statements made at the Council of Trent, like those of any council, have a quite specific historical setting; furthermore, at Trent possible correction from the Eastern churches was absent. In its final statements, according to its own words this Council only wanted to express what, according to its own understanding and interpretation, had been denied by the Reformers. This was also true in connection with the problem of the church's ministry. In the meantime the further course of history meant that the fathers of the Council of Trent simply had a summary and sometimes misguided conception of what had really happened at the Reformation. Thus – in accordance with the actual aim of this assembly of the Western church – the resolutions of this Council were only counter-positions; they are silent at the points over which the fathers of the Council were at one with Reformation positions. So we cannot look to Trent for a complete doctrine of the Catholic conception of the ministry, not even as it was held at that time. The resolutions are deliberately one-sided with respect to what the fathers of the Council themselves thought about the ministry. To give just one example: in its canons on the sacrament of ordination this council connects the ministry of the church ('priesthood', as what presbyters and bishops have in common) almost exclusively with presiding at the eucharist (the power of consecrating and performing other sacramental actions), whereas on the other hand in the reforming decrees (which were concerned more with reforming the clergy than directly challenging the Reformation) pastoral direction and proclamation were seen as the primary task of the priestly episcopate.[74] This apparent inconsistency can only be understood in the light of the strict intention of the canons of Trent, viz., of simply formulating opposing positions where in the view of the church fathers the Reformation either denies certain primal Christian traditions connected with the ministry or allows them to become obscured.

Conciliar authority lies in the final text of the Council of Trent as it has come down to us, and not what the fathers engaged in the council may have thought personally, and may even in fact have stated in the two sessions preceding the solemn session. Of course we cannot estimate the historical and theological significance of a particular council without critical study of the Acts of the three sessions in which the sacrament of ordination was discussed. However, it would be unrealistic to ignore the influence and after-effects of the Tridentine *doctrina* and *canones* as they appeared in their final version in the period following the Council of Trent. For these canons, too, made a specific contribution to a one-sided hardening of the conception of the ministry in the second millennium. It was these canons which made history, and not (or rather not yet) what critical historical hermeneutics over the last twenty years has discovered about the real purposes of the Council of Trent. Anyone who is familiar with the Acts of this Council can say that despite differences which are nevertheless real, and cannot be brushed aside, as a purely Latin Council the Council of Trent nevertheless in many respects both honoured views from the first millennium and equally anticipated views from the later Second Vatican Council. However, this justifiable historical view of Trent is markedly different from the actual historical consequences of the Council. Anyone who wants to evaluate the historical relevance of a Council must take account of both sides of the coin if they are not to be naive or unrealistic, or to reduce dogmatic theology to apologetics.

Furthermore, in its canons on the ministry, the Council of Trent did not want to adopt any position in connection with themes over which the Scotists, the Thomists and the Augustinians – the three great Catholic movements in this Council – were in mutual disagreement. Now these differences related not only to the substance of the sacrament of ordination and the relationship of presbyters to bishops, but also to the role of the believing people in the mandate of the church or the calling of candidates to the priesthood; they also related to the significance, the content and the extent of the so-called 'priestly character' – to mention just a few controversial matters! Thus very little was left that could actually be defined. In other words, given the fundamental task which the Council had set itself, the final result was inevitably going to seem 'poor' over against the rich and varied ideas (albeit narrowed down by their mediaeval context) which were current among the fathers of the Council. This poor final result is noticeable if we compare the canons of Trent, from the third session (15 July 1563), with what theologians and bishops had said about the ministry in the first session devoted to it (1557), in which Luther's views on the ministry were the chief subject for study, and in the second session (1551–1552), in which Calvin's views also came up. Only once was a bishop heard to lament that what was regarded by everyone 'as heresy' would be better countered by a positive, synthetic account of the Catholic view of the ministry than by fragmentary positions taken up against the Reformation.[75]

It is wrong to say that the way in which the Canons of Trent are directed against the Reformation is the reason why since then the 'priesthood' has almost exclusively been seen in connection with presiding at the eucharist (the power of consecration). That was already an earlier, mediaeval position (see above), against which the Reformation was in part a right reaction. In the Tridentine counter-reaction, this mediaeval view in fact gained one-sided importance, and that was the way in which this council later began to function. Furthermore, I have already explained how in early mediaeval theology the meaning of *corpus verum* (the church) and *corpus mysticum* (the eucharistic body of Christ) were seen as being opposed, a fact over which this Council (in so far as any of this semantic shift was perceived at Trent) was evidently at its wits' end. The relationship of the ministry to Christ on the one hand and to the church on the other was kept very vague by this Council, in a disappointing way; at the time of this session there was still no worked-out 'ecclesiology', while the experience of the community at that time (see the reforming decrees) left a good deal to be desired. Furthermore, the fact that Trent rightly also had to combat the attempts of the nobility – at that time the laity were the ones who had the power – to nominate bishops and priests led the Council (sometimes under the protests of a number of theologians) to reduce the role of the community of believing people virtually to nothing in the nominating of its ministers. This historical background to the Council of Trent does not do away with the fact that the view of the church held by this Council, deriving from feudal times, was very strongly hierarchical (Pope, bishops, priests, deacons and then – far below – the believing people).

Finally, the eight canons concerning the sacrament of ordination[76] are a reaction against a view which reduces the priest to a preacher, spokesman and proclaimer (with the result that at least in defining the functions of the priest the canons only stress his cultic activity and do not say anything about the tasks of preaching and teaching, which were stressed so strongly by scripture and the early church as the task of ministers of the church). In their final version the canons are also silent on the universal priesthood of believers, about which theologians and bishops had spoken so much in the first two sessions, evidently because mention of it could only play into the hands of the Reformation; however, the fathers of the Council in no sense denied this datum of scripture and the early church. Not once does Trent define what is the precise nature of the church's ministry or the sacrament of ordination, because Thomists and Scotists held differing views on the matter. The Scotists believed the sacramental character of consecration to lie in the 'rite of consecration' (at that time in fact the laying on of hands with anointing); the Thomists stressed, rather, the impression of the 'permanent sacrament': the state of being ordained, on the basis of the character and the powers which were acquired. These powers could be withdrawn, but not the character. In the final version, the hierarchical structure of the church (bishops, pres-byters and deacons), first formulated as a divine institution (*divina institutions*) is reduced to a divine ordinance (*divina or-dinatione*: in his providence God allowed historical develop-ments to take this course.)[77]

In most instances the Council defended the actual structures of the ministry as they had developed in the tradition and were then advocated by church authorities as church order. Here it defended directly less the developed structures in themselves (now and then the Council fathers show signs of being aware of historical changes in the structures of the ministry) than the authority of the church to define its own church order (which is now accepted ecumenically by all churches).[78] Thus the Tri-dentine decree on the ministry is less dogmatic than it seems; it defends the *de facto* church order. The historical consequences of this defence by the Council of the church order in force at the time, and the absence of a real theology of the ministry, was that in actual fact the Council simply took over the me-diaeval deviation in the conception and practice of the ministry and fundamentally strengthened it, though not deliberately; it sanctioned this deviation without intending to do so. Further-more, the sharp distinction between the power of consecration and the power of jurisdiction made it difficult for the fathers of the Council of Trent to gain a clear view of the ministry. Here the absence of the Eastern churches also made its effect, to the detriment of the Council. The legalistic narrowing down of the mediaeval view of the priest is in fact the result of all this. In the twentieth century, in particular Pius X, Pius XI and Pius XII contributed a great deal towards the popularizing of this narrow view of the priest,[79] which for many Christians down to the present day is a determining factor in their view of the priest.

It also determines the attitude of the official church towards the present shortage of priests. On all sides we hear of new patterns of behaviour which are inspired by that view of the priesthood. Generally speaking, they run like this: in view of the growing shortage of priests, let us engage as many lay people as possible in the pastoral work of the church (which in itself is a praiseworthy suggestion). In doing this, let us be loyal ourselves: let the laity do everything for which they have skills and a charisma. But, it is not for them to preside at the eucharist, in the ministry of reconciliation and at least in the sacramental last rites – in other words in sacramental institutions. All this is reserved for those on whom, as celibate candidates for the priesthood, the *sacra potestas*, the sacred power of consecration, has been bestowed. This *sacerdotium* or priesthood makes not just anyone, but only 'him' – a man – share in a special way in the high priesthood of Christ, for ordinary priests in a rather less powerful way than for those who hold the power of bishops. In this view, the priest is a mediator between Christ and the community in the presence of the Christian community. This priestly mediation, which makes the person who has been consecrated an *alter Christus*, rests on a character that the priest, without any merit on his part, nevertheless has in his personal possession by virtue of the holy power of the one who consecrates him and lays hands on him. In that case the priest has a power which he can also exercise on his own, even if the whole of the community is absent (unless the church forbids him to). (Even films are based on this 'absolute' power of consecration.) Furthermore, this power cannot be lost. As Graham Greene wrote in one of his novels, it works 'like an inoculation'.

Many of us thought that this was even a dogma of the church. In that connection it must be said that what I have just sketched out is not a Christian dogma, but broadly speaking the official teaching of the Western, Latin church. Given the practice and the views of the first Christian millennium, it cannot possibly be an unchangeable datum. Were this in fact to be the case, it would mean that for ten centuries the church had sanctioned a heretical practice, or, conversely, that the sixth canon of Chalcedon contained a flat condemnation of the influence of the canons of the Council of Trent on the ministry. In that case it would be a matter for dispute whether it was the first or the second Christian millennium which had the right to claim to be Christian and apostolic.

III

Continuity and Divergence between the First and Second Christian Millennia

1. The ecclesial and pneuma-christological basis of ministry, which later becomes a direct christological basis

It can be seen from the preceding analysis that, generally speaking, in church history it is possible to recognize three views of the priest (which are partly socially conditioned): patristic, feudal or mediaeval, and modern. Because views of human nature and social sensibility have changed, present-day criticism is principally directed at the modern view of the priest, and in its reaction this criticism shows a clear affinity to the image of the priest in the ancient church.

Although the theology of the ministry which has developed since the end of the twelfth and the beginning of the thirteenth century has its own Western, Latin features, in theological terms I can see two submerged lines of continuity in the great tradition of two thousand years' experience of the Christian ministry. On the one hand, not only the ancient and mediaeval but also the modern church oppose any celebration of the eucharist which denies the universal *communio ecclesialis*; and on the other hand, there is an ancient and modern awareness that no Christian community can call itself autonomously the ultimate source of its own ministers. Of course it has to be conceded that the first Christian millennium − above all in the pre-Nicene period − expressed its view of the ministry chiefly in ecclesial and pneumatological terms, or better pneuma-christologically, whereas the second Christian millennium gave the ministry a directly christological basis and shifted the mediation of the church into the background. In this way a theology of the ministry developed without an ecclesiology, just as in the Middle Ages the so-called treatise on the sacraments followed immediately on christology without the intervention of an independent ecclesiology (which at that stage had not yet been worked out). Although Thomas, at least, still always talks of 'sacraments of the church' (*sacramenta ecclesiae*), the sacrament will later be defined in a technical and abstract sense as *signum efficax gratiae*, in which the ecclesial dimension remains completely unconsidered. Its sacramental power is founded directly on the 'sacred' power (*sacra potestas*) which is the priest's personal possession. In this way the ecclesial significance of the ministry with its charismatic and pneumatological dimensions is obscured, and the more time goes on, the more the ministry is embedded in a legalistic cadre which bestows sacred power.

At many points Vatican II deliberately referred back to the theological intuitions of the ancient church, but its view of the church's ministry, above all in the terminology it used, is unmistakably a compromise between these two great blocks of tradition in the church.[1] The churchly or ecclesial dimension of the ministry is again stressed, and instead of *potestas* the council prefers to use the terms *ministeria* and *munera*: church service. However, *potestas sacra* also occurs several times, though the classic difference between *potestas ordinis* and *potestas iurisdictionis* cannot be found anywhere in *Lumen Gentium*. Rather, a break is made with this division, since it is stated that the essential foundation of the jurisdiction is already given with 'consecration' itself. Thus at least in principle, the old view of the *titulus ecclesiae* of the ministry is restored to favour, and at least a beginning is made towards breaking down the legalism which surrounds the ministry.

By contrast, however, in 1976, especially in the declaration by the Congregation of the Doctrine of Faith on women in the ministry, this conciliar equilibrium which had been regained is again distorted. Granted, the declaration concedes that the priest is the figure with which the community identifies, but it immediately adds that he has this status because first and foremost he represents Christ himself and also represents the church simply because he represents Christ as the head of the church.[2] Here the ecclesial and pneumatological standpoint is abandoned and the priesthood is again given a direct christological foundation.

On the basis of theological criteria I think that preference must be given to the first Christian millennium as a model for a future shaping of the church's ministry – albeit in a very different, modern historical context – and in particular to the New Testament and the pre-Nicene period. In arguing in this way I am also taking account of the Agreed Statements which have been put forward by official ecumenical commissions of theologians over the last ten years.[3] In the community of Jesus Christ, not everything is possible at will. The self-understanding of the Christian churches as the 'community of God' is the all-embracing principle. Therefore I shall first sum up the basic Christian view of the ministry in the church in a number of key concepts, taking account generally of modern, theological criticism of the ministry.

2. Towards an ecumenical consensus over the ministry in a 'community of Christ'

(a) *The specific character of the ministry within other services performed by and in the community*

Given the responsibility of all believers for the whole of the community, which also involves a whole series of other ministries and charismata, in the church there are also official ministerial services with their *own specific* feature, which is that they are different forms of pastoral *leadership* of the community or presiding over the community. Following an appropriate procedure, these ministers are themselves chosen by the community for this ministry, or are in fact confirmed by the community in their already existing position on the basis of their actual function in the community, a function marked by charismatic gifts. The call by the community is the specific ecclesial form of the call by Christ. Ministry from below is ministry from above.

After the apostolic period, but still within the New Testament, the custom already begins to arise in some communities of giving this calling by the community a liturgical form: in the last resort, the church does not make appointments as they are made to Unilever or General Motors, nor is this appointment like an appointment in the name of the civil authority. Hence the laying on of hands by leaders who at that time were still charismatic (first 'prophets', and later presbyters), with prophetic prayer, the later *epiclesis* to the Spirit. In short, it is the liturgical and sacramental expression of the sense of the community that what happens in the *ecclesia* is a gift of God's Spirit and not an expression of the autonomy of the church. Thus the *pneuma hēgemonikon* was called down on the real leader of the pastoral team of a local church (in the ancient church, historically speaking this was the bishop): the Spirit which directs the church community and also brings to mind what Jesus said and did, as it has been handed down to the communities as a heritage to be preserved in dynamic form through the apostolic tradition. It follows from this that as leader of the community the minister is the president at the eucharist, in which the community celebrates its deepest mystery and its own existence, in thanksgiving and praise to God.

The team leader is assigned fellow workers in his ministry, who are similarly appointed through the laying on of hands and prayer, in which it is said in rather vaguer or more specific ways to what specialized ministry they have been summoned. The charisma which they need for their particular ministry is called down on them. However, by virtue of the spiritual charisma which they have been given, in emergencies all ministers can take the place of the team leader and perform his ministry without supplementary 'ordinations' being needed. It is often difficult to define where official and non-official ministry begins or ends in the specific life of a community. However, to put it briefly, the concepts of leadership, instruction, liturgy or diaconate show what the great Christian tradition understood as official ministry. Still, the New Testament allows the church every freedom in the specific structures of the ministry; even the choice of an episcopal or presbyteral church order is not a schismatic factor in the light of the New Testament. Church history also points in the same direction. Apart from the fact that the mono-episcopacy of the Ignatian writings must now be put much later than people had hitherto thought, many mediaeval theologians, above all the Thomists, did not see the distinction between episcopate and presbyterate as a difference in the power of consecration but only in the power of jurisdiction, while Thomas at the same time could nevertheless say that the episcopate 'is the source of all church ministries'.[4] This question remained a focal point of vigorous controversy for a whole century, until on 20 October 1756, in his letter *In Postremo*, Pope Benedict XIV allowed the theologians complete freedom. Furthermore, it cannot be said that the Second Vatican Council settled this question in principle. On the contrary, this council gives a synthetic theology of *de facto* church order, in which the episcopacy is assigned 'the fullness of the priesthood'.[5] In actual church order, then, the presbyterate is a matter of sharing in the priesthood of the bishops; presbyters are 'auxiliary priests'. However, we cannot say that this is actual dogma.

According to the New Testament, in the first place it is Christ and the church who are priestly; nowhere in the New Testament does the minister in the church take on particularly priestly characteristics. Even Augustine, who recognizes the priestly character of the minister, opposes a theology which sees the minister as a mediator between Christ and humanity. As a consequence of the priestly character of Christ and his church it is also correct to apply the adjective 'priestly' to the minister in his service to Christ and his church; he is the servant of and in the priestly community of, and in association with, Christ the priest. However, at this point we should not forget that even the Second Vatican Council did not explicitly want to use one formula proposed, viz., the priest as the mediator between Christ and the faithful.

(b) Clergy and laity

At a very early stage after the New Testament, with Clement, a distinction arose between *klerikos* and *laikos*, analogous to the Jewish distinction between 'high priest and the people' (Isa. 42.2; Hos. 4.9),[6] but this terminology in no way indicates a difference of status between laity and clergy. A *klerikos* is someone who has a *kleros*, i.e. a ministry.[7] What we have here, therefore, is a distinction of function, not in an official civic sense, but in an ecclesial sense; however, there were charismatic functions in the church which were of a specific kind compared with other ministries in the community. In this light, given the whole of the church's tradition, the insertion in *Lumen Gentium* – which is in fact a quotation from an encyclical of Pius XII – in which it is said that the ordained priesthood is 'essentially different' (*essentia differunt*) from the priesthood of the believing people of God (the Reformers' phrase 'universal ministry' also seems to me to be inappropriate terminology) must be interpreted as the confirmation of a specific and indeed sacramental function and not as a state.[8] Because of this, and in my view correctly, the term hierarchy is not used in an ecumenical context to denote ministries; however, this is in no way to undervalue the function of leadership and authority in the church. Even the great mediaeval theologians refuse to speak of the ministry in terms of *praelatio* and *subiectio*: 'this is not meant by the *sacramentum ordinis*'.[9] The tension between an ontological-sacerdotalist view of the ministry on the one hand and a purely functionalist view on the other must therefore be resolved by a theological view of the church's ministry as a charismatic office, the service of leading the community, and therefore as an ecclesial function within the community and accepted by the community. Precisely in this way it is a gift of God.

(c) Sacramental ministry

The sacramentality (which is non-sacral) of the ministry emerges from what has just been said; it is normally coupled with initiation through a liturgical celebration.[10] Although at present the ecumenical discussion of the technical meaning of the word 'sacrament' is certainly not finished, in point of content all Christian churches which accept the ministry in the church are agreed over what may be regarded as the essential elements of *ordinatio*: calling (or acceptance) by the community and appointment to or for a community. The normal, specific form of this laid down by church order is the laying on of hands by other ministers with the offering of the *epiclesis* by all concerned;[11] in this respect the Catholic church is not alone. At present, therefore, ecumenical theology rightly no longer connects the question of mutual acceptance at the eucharist with the question of the recognition of each other's ministry. As, for example, the analysis by the Greek Orthodox theologian J. D. Zizioulas has shown,[12] the sacramental ministry is the action in which the community realizes itself; for him too, the charisma (without any contrast between 'ministry' and institution) is essentially the *ordinatio*, but as something which concerns the community of the church, as a gift of the Spirit with both a sacramental and legal dimension. Here the validity of consecration is bound up not so much with one isolated sacramental action of the church, i.e. the liturgical laying on of hands seen in itself, as with the action of an apostolic church community as a whole.[13] Within this view, 'extraordinary forms of ministry' as expressed in the Bible and the early church are to be given a positive evaluation by the church in special circumstances.

(d) Sacramental character

For some Christian churches the sacramental character[14] of the ministry still remains a stumbling block. This should not be the case. The first official church document which mentions a character dates from 1201 (the character of baptism, in a letter written by Pope Innocent III): 'the priestly character' appears for the first time in 1231 in a letter from Gregory IX to the Archbishop of Paris.[15] In its doctrine of the character, from the beginning of the thirteenth century on, high scholasticism had above all stressed the link between the 'sacrament of ordination' and the 'church', following the ancient church, though using a new conceptual category. Of course the sacerdotalist-ontological

conception of the ministry which had grown up in the meantime
was also connected with the character, which after a number of
centuries would have to support all the weight of the ontologizing view of the ministry. From a dogmatic point of view,
however, all that had been formulated was the existence of the
character; of course, Trent wanted to leave open all precise
explanations of it, even the view of some that it was merely the
relatio rationis or logical relationship (Durant de Saint Pourçain).
In other words, the ontologizing approach cannot be based on
the councils which speak of character.[16] In the last resort 'character' seems to be a particular mediaeval category which expressed the ancient church's view of the permanent relationship
between the minister and the gift of the pneumatological charisma of ministry in the church. In the Middle Ages a distinction
was then made in this charisma of ministry between the authority of the entrusted office (expressed, moreover, in terms
of *potestas sacra*) and the sacramental grace appropriate to it,
which equipped the minister to exercise authority in a personally holy and truly Christian way. This distinction played into
the hands of ontological sacerdotalizing.[17] According to
II Tim. 1.6, however, the minister receives a charisma of ministry in the service of the community; here all the attention is
focussed on the charismatic and spiritual character of the ministry. In this the minister follows Jesus: in the spirituality and
ethics of the gospel.

(e) *The community and its celebration of the eucharist*

The ancient church and (above all since Vatican II) the modern
church cannot envisage any Christian community without the
celebration of the eucharist. There is an essential link between
local *ecclesia* and eucharist. Throughout the pre-Nicene church
it was held, evidently on the basis of Jewish models, that a
community in which at least twelve fathers of families were
assembled had the right to a priest or community leader and
thus to the eucharist, at which he presided.[18] In the small communities, these originally episcopal leaders soon became presbyteral leaders, pastors. In any case, according to the views of
the ancient church a shortage of priests was an ecclesiastical
impossibility. The modern so-called shortage of priests therefore
stands to be criticized in the light of the ancient church's view
of church and ministry, because the modern shortage in fact
has causes which stem from outside the ministry, namely the
conditions with which the ministry has already been associated

a priori, on not specifically ecclesiological grounds. Even now there are more than enough Christians, men and women, who in ecclesiological and ministerial terms possess this charisma, e.g. many catechists in Africa, and men and women pastoral workers in Europe and elsewhere; or who are at least prepared for appointment to the ministry if they do not feel that that means being clericalized and having to enter the service of a 'system'. According to the norms of the early church they meet every requirement.[19]

(f) Local and universal church

Finally, there is the relationship between ministry in a local church and ministry in the 'universal church'. In the ancient world, the universal church was not an entity above the local churches. To begin with there was no supra-regional organization, though patriarchates and metropolitan churches soon developed, in which various local churches were brought together in a supra-provincial unity. As time went on, increasing recognition was given in the course of the first five centuries to the patriarchal *Sedes Romana*, the seat of Peter, as a result of the 'primacy of the bond of love', even the other great patriarchates.[20]

Vatican II once again took up the ancient notion of the universal church. The Council speaks of the local church communities 'in which the one, holy, catholic, and apostolic Church of Christ is truly present and operative'.[21] The universal church is present in accentuated form in the local church. The view of Karl Rahner, who sees the universal church in the 'higher, supra-diocesan personnel in the church', who form the College of Bishops, has no basis either in the factual history of the church or in Vatican II. Rather, people belong to the universal church because they belong to a local community.[22] For this reason, however, no single community can monopolize the Spirit of God; as a result, mutual criticism on the basis of the gospel is possible within the local communities. Christian solidarity with other communities is an essential part of even the smallest grass-roots church communities. This ecclesial concern cannot be referred to higher authorities. It is a concern of every church community, but that should not include *a priori* self-censorship, in the sense that people exclude from the start everything that would not be welcome to higher authorities, though they themselves see it as legitimate Christian practice and as possible and urgently necessary within the context of their own church life. Within an 'integrated leadership' ultimate responsibility is left to the person who in fact bears it; otherwise an obstructive vicious circle develops within the collegial leadership in the church. It was to overcome such introversion that the spokesmen of neighbouring communities were required to be present at the liturgical institution of ministers in a particular local community.

All confessions in fact accept a supra-parochial and supra-diocesan ministry, in the sense of a synod, in a personal *episcopē*, in conferences of bishops, and even in the papacy. However, the structure is such that local ministers, as critical spokesmen of their churches, at the same time concern themselves with the management of the 'universal church', the bond of love, along with the one from among them who fulfils the function of Peter. I think that a growing ecumenical consensus has emerged in all this.

IV

Tension between Actual Church Order and Alternative Practices in the Ministry

1. Church order as a historically conditioned means of salvation

It emerges from the historical theological sketch which I have given that the constant in the church's ministry is always to be found only in specific, historically changing forms. In this evaluation I am beginning from the insight that is really shared by all Christians: that church order, though changing, is a very great benefit for Christian communities. In one form or another church order is part of the specific and essential manifestation of the 'communities of God', the church. However, this church order is not an end in itself. Like the ministry, it too is at the service of the apostolic communities and may not be made an end in itself, or be absolutized. That is all the more the case because it is evident that at all periods of the church it is utterly bound up with a specific conditioned history. At a particular point in history, moreover, certain forms of church order (and thus also criteria for the admission of ministers), called into being by earlier situations in the church and in society, come up against their limitations; this can also be demonstrated in sociological terms. These limitations can clearly be shown in terms of specific experiences of their shortcomings and faults, in other words, from negative experiences with a particular church order in changed circumstances. With a shift in the dominant picture of man and the world, with social and economic changes and a new social and cultural sensibility and set of emotions, a church order which has grown up through history can in fact hinder and obstruct precisely what in earlier times it was intended to ensure: the building up of a Christian community. Experiences of contrast then give rise to spontaneous experiments in possibilities of new forms of life for Christianity and the church (which also happened in New Testament Christianity). Experiences of defects in a given system in fact have a regulative force. Of course even a largely unanimous experience of what has gone wrong within a valid system which has grown up through history by no means amounts to agreement over the positive steps that must be taken. The specific direction in which things can change can only emerge from tests made through a large number of models, some of which will succeed and some fail. These can and may also fail; they are precise experiments with that possibility in view. Failure is nothing to be ashamed of, but a phase within the quest for a new discovery of Christianity. In these manifold attempts the binding character of the new possibilities for Christian life and the life of the church, which have been brought to life but still not given a completely specific form, will gradually become evident. This will happen in the case of the ministry also.

On the other hand it is also a sociological fact that in changed times there is a danger that the existing church order will become a fixed ideology, above all by reason of the inertia of an established system which is therefore often concerned for self-preservation. This is true of any system in society, but perhaps in a special way of the institutional church, which, rightly understanding itself as a 'community of God', often wrongly shows a tendency to identify even old and venerable traditions with unchangeable divine ordinances. Here Vatican II was more careful than people perhaps thought at the time. Whereas at the Council of Trent (see above) there was at least a suggestion that the tripartite division of the ministry into episcopate, presbyterate and diaconate went back to divine law, the Second Vatican Council replaced the *ordinatione divina* ('through divine dispensation') which had already been weakened at Trent, by the still more relativistic 'it was like this from antiquity'.[1]

2. Illegality

Thus against the background of the existing church order, new and perhaps urgently necessary alternative possibilities can usually be seen only through the medium of what must provisionally be called 'illegality'. This is not a new phenomenon in the church; things have always been that way. Furthermore, the old, mediaeval scholasticism, which was still very free (in contrast to later scholasticism, which ignored this fact), sometimes elevated this provisional illegality to the status of a theological principle, especially in its theory of the *non-acceptatio legis*, the rejection of the law-from-above by opposition from the grass roots. Whatever the value of the law may be, in particular instances it is rejected by a great majority and therefore in fact is irrelevant. Thus from the history of the church it seems that there is a way in which Christians can develop a practice in the church from below, from the grass-roots, which for a time can compete with the official practice recognized by the church, but which in its Christian opposition and illegality can eventually nevertheless become the dominant practice of the church, and finally be sanctioned by the official church (whereupon the whole process can begin all over again, since time never stands still). That is how things have always been!

What each of us hears about practices in the ministry which diverge from the official church order therefore: 1. has a diagnostic and dynamic effect, and serves to criticize ideology: and 2. itself has a normative power. This latter is not, of course, on the basis of the fact that these alternative practices actually exist. It is to be justified by the nature of Christianity, in that on the one hand they anticipate the future in a utopian way and on the other hand they express a Christian apostolic conviction which is to be tested by the whole history of Christian experience.

The normative force of facts as such – 'hard facts', as the sociologists say – reigns supreme in our secular, bourgeois society. But none of us would claim that facts or statistics in themselves have any normative authority. Such a position would in fact be a blunder, because it would also and even *a fortiori* have to attribute even more massive authority to the even greater factual dimension of the church order which exists at present. But just as the official church order must be justified in the face of the ups and downs of the historical experiences of Christians, and in our time in the face of the negative way in which Christians experience this church order, so too must the critical, new alternative forms of practice in the church and in the ministry also be justified over against our historical experiences. An alternative, or the new for its own sake, is nothing. A particular practice of the Christian community, whether old or new, always has authority only in so far as it is indwelt by the Christian 'logos', that is, by what I have called the apostolicity of the Christian community. Furthermore, 'All things are lawful, but not all things are helpful' (Paul).

Historically, accounts of new, alternative practices in Christianity and the church are always connected with reminiscences and experiences of what is faulty and sometimes even absurd in the existing system: with the obstructions which are in fact there. In assessing the authority of an alternative practice it is certainly possible to begin from present-day experiences of the situation: from demands made in the name of humanity, human rights and so on. This is a legitimate and even obvious way. However, because of the experiences I have been through, and in view of the toughness of any system, I have preferred to adopt another way which also seems to me to be a more strategic one, namely to choose as my starting point what has been accepted and defended by both sides of the church with a view to building up the Christian community: both by representatives of the official church order, which is still in force, and by the protagonists of the critical, alternative practice. To put it briefly, this is the right of the Christian community by itself to do everything necessary to be a true community of Jesus and to be able to develop itself intensively, albeit in connection with and in the light of mutual criticism from all other Christian communities. This situation can lead to genuine restrictions both from above and from below (Vatican II). To make the same point in a more limited way: this is the right of the community to the eucharist as the heart of the community (Vatican II). Alternatively, it is the apostolic right of the community to have leaders: i.e., a leader (male or female) or a 'significant other figure' who, on the basis of the fundamental values of the group, clarifies, dynamizes and also is able to criticize the community, and in so doing can also be subject to the criticism of the community. Fundamentally, the official church also accepts these apostolic affirmations, but at the same time in this respect it begins from decisions which have already been made at a prior stage of history (e.g. on criteria for admission to the ministry). However, when circumstances change in the church and the world, these can in fact obstruct this original right which belongs to the community. Thus, for example, the present shortage of priests (which itself can partly already be explained in terms of pre-existing historical conditions) leads to all kinds of substitute forms of church ministries. Alongside an authentic multiplicity of ministries which have become necessary because of the present-day situation of the community, i.e. the more differentiated ministry in the church, there is also an inauthentic multiplicity – simply because consecration or sacramental accreditation has in fact been withheld.

This approach, in terms of what is commonly accepted, serves to show more clearly the dilemma in which the so-called modern view of the priest now finds itself. On these grounds it must have become clear to everyone that in modern conditions, for example, the actual celebration of the eucharist has come up against fundamental difficulties; it is sometimes trivialized and often completely blocked. A whole series of accounts of negative experiences which have been brought about by the actual functioning of the 'service' priest within a sacral vision of the ministry shows that at the moment this view of the priesthood often makes the community and the eucharist look utterly ridiculous in the context of Christianity and the church. And this happens when there is an abundance of pastoral workers, men and women, who sometimes have already spent many years in full-time work for the community. These negative experiences make it quite clear that the actual order of the church has now become fixed as an ideology and itself hinders the original purpose of the church. And the only reason for this problem over the sacraments is the absence of a male, celibate priest – both non-theological concepts. Many Christians can simply no longer take this. Consequently such negative experiences are an occasion for particular Christians and their ministers for the moment to take it into their own hands to begin an alternative practice. This is the reason why the phenomenon of an alternative form of ministry, which is in fact making itself felt everywhere, serves to provide a diagnosis of symptoms of sickness in the existing system, and in addition functions as a criticism of the ideology which is bound up with traditional practices. For many Christians it has become clear meanwhile that the alternative practice is a clear expression of the New Testament datum of the priority of the community over the ministry (and *a fortiori* over criteria for admission to the ministry which are not necessary in themselves). Furthermore, it is a sociological fact that existing ordinances in a particular society, even when that society is the church, remain intact as long as they carry intrinsic conviction, i.e. as long as no one doubts their (Christian) 'logos' or 'reason'. In itself, the fact that at a particular moment a wave of alternative practices sweeps over the church throughout the world indicates that the existing church order has lost a structure of credibility and is in urgent need of being revised. For many believers it no longer carries any conviction, so that spontaneously, and on all sides, we find the social and psychological mechanism of the *non-acceptatio legis*. This is what we now in fact see happening on a large scale. If despite this the church wants to maintain its existing church order, then from this point it can do so only in an authoritarian fashion (because it carries no conviction with a great many 'subjects').

This course would simply make the situation more precarious, because in turn the authoritarian way of exercising authority conflicts with the basic themes of the way in which life is experienced today, and is also experienced by Christians.

Finally, this alternative practice also has a dynamizing effect. At any rate, particular Christians are gradually recognizing the new structure of credibility; furthermore, as time goes on, they come to identify with it more and more. It is not the bare fact of an alternative way of exercising ministry which has dynamic force, but the way in which, by virtue of the 'Christian reason' which can be found in it, Christians almost infallibly recognize a modern form of 'apostolicity' here. It is precisely because a new practice of this kind carries conviction that in the long run it acquires authority and the power to attract. Nevertheless, we cannot claim that this experienced conviction, which now already inspires and determines the lives of many communities and ministers even before it has been recognized openly by the official church, does not possess an inherent Christian apostolicity, and can only acquire this when it is sanctioned by the church at a later stage. On the contrary, it is recognized later when, and in so far as, it already has in fact an innate Christian 'logos' or apostolicity: when it in fact provides the possibility for a meaningful Christian life today.

3. The traditional reception of practices which diverge from church order

Through the long history of its experience, the Western church has also had to refer to all kinds of principles on the basis of which practices that diverge from existing church order might nevertheless be regarded as being 'in order'.

First of all there is the principle of the 'extraordinary minister', which sanctioned what was often originally an 'illegal practice'. According to the anti-Donatist Council of Arles (314), in the absence of priests, deacons may preside at the eucharist;[2] at the time of the persecution of Diocletian (303–311) they replaced not only priests but bishops. Furthermore, it is known that for more than a century, abbots consecrated priests, with papal permission.[3] We can say that in addition to the 'ordinary minister' (in terms of church order) there have always in the end also been 'extraordinary ministers' for the administration of virtually all the sacraments.

Another principle of the Western church is above all the *supplet Ecclesia*.[4] This applies particularly in the case of mistakes in form, in which the sacrament has not been administered in accordance with the rules of church order. Here the church as it were compensates for these lacunae. From the history of this practice since the Middle Ages it seems that the Latin church appeals to this question less in cases of the absence of the power of consecration (*potestas ordinis*), and above all when it is a matter of the absence of the power of jurisdiction (which has clearly been distinguished from the power of consecration in the Latin church from the Middle Ages to the Second Vatican Council – in contrast to the Eastern churches).

There is also the principle of *intentio faciendi quod facit Ecclesia*.[5] Here someone can have the intention of wanting to do what the church does (e.g. baptize) though without in fact taking account of the form prescribed by church order. In this case, too, the action is valid in terms of both Christianity and the church. This means that there are traces of the sacramental church outside the area dominated by its church order, e.g. in marginal 'grass-roots communities' which have sometimes grown up outside the sphere of authority of the bishop. Although these stand apart from existing church order, they nevertheless seek to be in the great tradition of the church.

The appeal to a *sanatio in radice* (healing at the roots), and above all a reference to the power of dispensation held by the church authorities, is specifically connected with the theory of the *plena potestas* which has emerged since the Middle Ages. This relates to the powers which the Pope in particular is said to possess, so that in the last resort he can diverge from all church order currently obtaining (albeit within certain limits).[6] Despite any illegality in respect of existing church order the Pope can subsequently declare what has been done as nevertheless valid. However, for the time being alternative grass-roots communities will not be able to make much of this principle.

Finally there is the ancient doctrine of the *non-receptio legis*, on the basis of which a church law, while being valid, can in the long run become irrelevant because it is in fact no longer accepted by the great majority of believers.[7] Laws only in fact have force if they are also supported by the community and have a plausible structure.

Most of these principles can in fact be invoked even in the case of a modern 'illegal' practice, which nevertheless respects the intention of the great church (in other words, which means to remain in line with the main church tradition). This is the case on one condition, which has been properly formulated by the Council of Trent: *salva eorum substantia*, in other words, provided that the 'substance of the sacrament' is preserved.[8] However, when it comes to the 'sacrament of consecration', the question has arisen as to precisely what belongs to the substance of the church's ministry and what does not (though the so-called 'substance' will always be found in a specific liturgical form, through which it is 'given substance'). Now it has emerged from the theology of the ministry in the first millenium that the sacramental substance or nucleus of *ordinatio*, appointment to an office, lies in the fact that as a minister a believer is recognized and accepted by the church (the local community and its leaders) and is called to the service of the ministry in and for a particular community, along with the gift of the Spirit which is bestowed in such an instance. The rights of a local church can of course be 'moderated' (above all by Pope and Council) with an eye to what the Latin church calls the *utilitas Ecclesiae* or the welfare of the church; however, this last is in that case part of historically changing church order, and not the substance of the sacrament concerned, so that here in particular instances an appeal can be made to the principles outlined above. Thus in 1088 Pope Urban II sanctioned deviations from existing church order with an eye to very specific situations in the church and the world.[9] However, quite apart from historical ecclesiastical rules for *communio* among all local churches, concern for this bond of love in the church is of the *substance* of each separate community. With these principles in mind we can now come to an evaluation of present-day alternative practices in respect of the ministry.

4. An evaluation of present-day alternative practices in the ministry

The alternative practice of critical communities which are inspired by Jesus as the Christ is 1. possible from an apostolic and dogmatic point of view (I cannot pass judgment on all the details here). It is a legitimate way of living a Christian life, commensurate with the apostolicity of the church, which has been called into being by the needs of the time. To talk of 'heretics' or those who 'already stand outside the church' (on grounds of this alternative practice) seems to me to be non-sensical from the church's point of view. Furthermore, 2. given the present canonical church order, the alternative practice is not in any way *contra* (against) *ordinem*; it is *praeter ordinem*. In other words, it does not follow the letter of existing church order (it is *contra* this letter), but it is in accordance with what church order really set out to safeguard (in earlier situations). It is understandable that such a situation is never pleasant for the representatives of existing church order. However, they too should take note of the negative experiences of Christians with church order and above all be sensitive to the damage which these do to the formation of communities, to the eucharist and to the ministry. Otherwise they are no longer defending the Christian community and its eucharistic heart and centre, but an established system, the purely factual dimension. At a time when people have become extra-sensitive to the power-structure of a system, a hardening of attitude in the existing system to the luxuriant upsurge of all kinds of experiments (even if some of them are perhaps frivolous) would be a very painful matter for all those who are well disposed towards the church.

Given that the alternative practice is not directly *contra ordinem*, but generally speaking merely *praeter ordinem*, in difficult circumstances in the church it can also be defended in an ethical respect (of course no one can pass judgment on subjective intentions). In this connection, too, to talk of 'members who have placed themselves outside the church' is not only a distressing phenomenon which has no place in the church, but also smacks of what the church itself has always called heresy. Even the Second Vatican Council had difficulty in defining where the limits of church membership really lie. Of course they can be found somewhere; but how can they be defined precisely? Furthermore, talk like this makes posthumous heretics of authentic Christians of earlier centuries and above all condemns the New Testament search for the best possibilities of pastoral work.

I also want to say here that no one may pursue this alternative practice in a triumphalist spirit: this also seems to me to be un-apostolic. It remains a provisionally abnormal situation in the life of the churches. Personally (but this is simply a very personal conviction) I think that there is also need for something like a strategy or 'economy of conflicts'. Where there is clearly no urgent necessity for an alternative practice because of a pastoral need felt by the Christian communities, ministers must not put into practice everything that is possible in apostolic or dogmatic terms. In that case, of course, there is a danger that, for example, in critical communities, the communities are again put in second place after the problems of the ministry and begin to be manipulated on the basis of problems arising from the crisis of identity among ministers themselves. In addition, we must not turn alternative forms of ministerial practice into a mystique. We need a degree of realism and matter-of-factness. Of course renewals in the church usually begin with illegal deviations; renewals from above are rare, and are sometimes dangerous. Vatican II is an illustration of both these points. In its Constitution on the Liturgy, this Council largely sanctioned the illegal liturgical practice which had grown up above all in France, Belgium and Germany. On the other hand, when after the Council the Vatican programme of renewal was put into effect in other matters, largely on promptings from above, many people proved to be unprepared, so that there was resistance in many communities.

One often hears the objection that changes or an alternative practice are not justified by the fact that they are different or new. That is quite correct; but the implicit presupposition here is wrong. In changed circumstances this is equally true of the existing church order. It too cannot be legitimated on the basis of the inertia of its own factual existence. When views of man or the world change, it too can come under the suspicion of deterioration, i.e. of actually falling short of authentic Christian and church life. Even the old and venerable does not enjoy any priority because it is old and venerable.

Some people will criticize my views for being too one-sided and seeing the church in 'horizontal' terms, exclusively in accordance with the model of a social reality which can be treated in sociological terms, and not as a charismatic datum 'from above'. I must reject this ecclesial dualism, on the basis of the New Testament. Of course we may not speak about the church only in descriptive empirical language; we must also speak about the church in the language of faith, of the church as the 'community of Jesus', as 'the body of the Lord', the 'temple of the Spirit', and so on. And this language of faith expresses a real dimension of the church. However, in both cases we are talking about one and the same reality: otherwise we should split up the church in a gnostic way into a 'heavenly part' (which would fall outside the sphere of sociological approaches) and an earthly part (to which all the bad features could evidently be transferred). Vatican II already reacted against this with the words: 'We may not see the earthly church and the church enriched with heavenly things as two realities' (*Lumen Gentium* I, 8). In my view, the obstacles to the renewal of the official ministry in the church are grounded above all in this dualistic conception of the church (which is often described in pseudo-Christian terms as 'hierarchical'). The consequence of this is that because of the shortage of priests Christian laity are allowed to engage in pastoral work as much as possible but are refused the sacramental institution to the ministry which goes with this. The question is more whether this development in the direction of pastoral workers (whose existence can only be understood in the light of the historical obstructions which have been placed in the way of the ministry) who are not ministers and have not been appointed sacramentally is a sound theological development. It maintains the exaggerated sacral view of the priesthood, as will emerge even more closely from what follows.

5. Celibacy as a charisma and the 'compulsory celibacy of the minister' (and related problems)

(a) Abstinence and celibacy

The law of celibacy, at first implicit in the Latin church at the First Lateran Council (1123) and then promulgated explicitly in canons 6 and 7 of the Second Lateran Council in 1139, was the conclusion of a long history in which there was simply a law of abstinence, applying to married priests. This earlier history extends from the end of the fourth century until the twelfth century. This history shows that the fundamental matter was a law of abstinence: the law of celibacy has grown out of a law of abstinence and was promulgated with the intention of making the law of abstinence effective.

In the New Testament period and in the early church there were from the start both married and unmarried ministers. The reasons why some of them remained unmarried might be personal, social or religious. Of course in the biblical post-apostolic period it is constantly stressed that ministers must be 'the husband of one wife' (I Tim. 3.2; 3.12; Titus 3.6), i.e. that they must love their wives devotedly. But there is no mention here of the impossibility of remarrying. At that time we often find on epitaphs, 'he was the husband of one wife', i.e. he loved his wife.

However, in the first centuries there was an increase in the number of priests who remained unmarried of their own free will, inspired by the same motives as monks. Only towards the end of the fourth century did there appear in the West completely new, ecclesiastical legislation concerned with married ministers (here bishops, presbyters and deacons). However, we have to wait until the Second Vatican Council before the church mentions Matt. 19.11f. in one of its canonical documents (which to begin with, discuss a temporary law of abstinence and later a permanent law of abstinence and finally the law of celibacy, in connection with the clergy). This passage talks of 'religious celibacy', i.e. 'for the sake of the kingdom of God', without any reference to ritual laws of purity (which were, of course, completely alien to Jesus).

Until a few years ago, this beginning of the law of abstinence was generally put at the beginning of the third century. Both the Council of Elvira (the beginning of the third century) and the Council of Nicaea, along with certain *Canones synodum Romanorum ad Gallos*, played a part here. However, since then historical criticism has definitively shown that canon 33 of the Spanish Council of Elvira, along with other parts of this assembly, has nothing to do with the council. This canon goes back to a collection from the end of the fourth century. Furthermore, we also have historical proof that an alleged discussion about the abstinence of priests never took place at the Council of Nicaea: this is a legend which came into being in the middle of the fifth century as a reaction from the East against the law of abstinence which had meanwhile been introduced in the West.[10] Furthermore, the collection of the *Canones ad Gallos* is so problematical that for the moment, because of doubts about chronology, we cannot draw any conclusions at all from them.

Thus the origin of the law of abstinence for married priests unmistakably lies in Rome at the end of the fourth century: the only question is whether it happened under Pope Damasus (366–384) or Pope Siricius (384–399).

It appears from these official documents that the dominant reason for the introduction of a law of abstinence is 'ritual purity'. In ancient times the Eastern and Western churches of the first ten centuries never thought of making celibacy a condition of entering the ministry: both married and unmarried men were welcome as ministers. Originally, i.e. from the end of the fourth century on, church law, which was at that time new, contained a *lex continentiae* (see e.g. PL 54, 1204). This was a liturgical law, forbidding sexual intercourse in the night before communicating at the eucharist. Furthermore, this custom had long been observed. However, when, in contrast to the Eastern churches, from the end of the fourth century the Western churches began to celebrate the eucharist daily, in practice this abstinence became a permanent condition for married priests.[11] A law to this effect became necessary for the first time at the end of the fourth century, and there was canonical legislation accordingly. What we have, then, is not a law of celibacy, but a law of abstinence connected with ritual purity, focussed above all on the eucharist. Despite this obligation to abstinence, married priests were forbidden to send away their wives; not only an obligation to abstinence but also living together in love with his wife was an obligation for the priest under canon law.[12]

The critical question posed by the New Testament is: how could Christians again allow the force of ancient laws of purity, when Jesus and the New Testament writers revoked the ritual precepts of the Old Testament and declared them void? For it is a fact that all church documents, down to and including the encyclical *Sacra Virginitas* of Pius XII (1954),[13] always refer to the Levitical laws of purity in connection with priestly celibacy (the main passages quoted are: Ex. 19.15; I Sam. 21.5–7; Lev. 15.16f.; 22.4).

We saw above that in the first centuries, as time went on, the ministry was increasingly compared with the Old Testament priesthood, so that the church's vocabulary of ministry became 'sacerdotalized'. However, while the allusion to Old Testament laws of purity could certainly evoke this, it could not make it acceptable to Christians. This acceptance can only be understood in the light of the general cultural climate of antiquity, above all in areas round the Mediterranean. In this Hellenistic area, which was also influenced by Eastern thought, laws of purity for pagan priests were very prominent: 'Anyone who approaches the altar must not have enjoyed the pleasures of Venus the night before',[14] a rule which can later be found in all Catholic liturgical books (though put in a more modest form). We can understand these ancient liturgical laws of abstinence in the light of the Stoic ideal of 'equanimity', which was widespread at that time (in antiquity sexual intercourse was called a 'little epilepsy', above all by the Stoics; it robs people of their senses and therefore is not 'in accord with reason'). Neo-Pythagoreanism and later, above all, Neo-Platonic dualism also played a part: the Neo-Platonist pagan Porphyry wrote a book entitled *On Abstinence*, which enjoyed great popularity at the time.[15] Christians, too, were children of their age, although they were critical of their pagan surroundings. In addition, we should not forget that to begin with there were Christian churches which regarded sexual abstinence as a baptismal obligation, which was therefore binding on all Christians.[16] And although the official church constantly and emphatically defended marriage against such views as being good and holy and a gift by God at creation, pressure from its pagan environment led it to be more reserved towards what was referred to as the 'use of marriage': this was only permissible for the purposes of procreation and even then any pleasure associated with it was regarded as being not quite right.

Thus at the origin of the law of abstinence and later the law of celibacy we find an antiquated anthropology and an ancient view of sexuality. *Omnis coitus immundus* was the way in which Jerome expressed the then universal view of pagans and Christians: 'sexual intercourse is impure'.[17]

Furthermore, when in the twelfth century the ritual law of abstinence was turned into a law of celibacy, this theme continued to remain the chief reason behind the actual law of the celibacy of ministers. The Second Lateran Council, in which this law is officially promulgated, puts the emphasis here: '*so that* the *lex continentiae* and the purity which is well-pleasing to God may extend among clergy and those who are ordained, we decree. . .';[18] the law of celibacy is explicitly seen as the drastic means of finally making the law of abstinence effective. It emerges clearly from the Councils between the fifth and the tenth centuries that the law of abstinence was observed only very superficially by married priests. The church authorities were aware of this.[19] After a variety of vain attempts to make it more strict by sanctions and 'economic' penalties they resorted to the most drastic means of all: a prohibition against marriage. Only from that time (1139) does marriage become a bar to the priesthood, so that only the unmarried could become priests.

I demonstrated above how in the first ten centuries many Christians were called upon to preside by the community against their inclination. Once complete abstinence was enjoined on priests in the West towards the end of the fourth century, we can see to what degree this extra burden led many priests into deplorable situations: these ancient councils bear abundant witness to this. In many cases at that time there was no question of abstinence freely accepted, certainly not as long as it was law that anyone could be called – and often was called – to preside over a community against his will.[20]

Even after the Second Lateran Council, the law of abstinence, and thus ritual purity, therefore remained the all-decisive and sole motive in the question of the 'obligatory celibacy' of priests. There is all the less mention here of a 'religious celibacy for the sake of the kingdom of God'. 'One does not approach the altar and the consecrated vessels "with soiled hands"': so went the pagan view which had now been taken over by the Christians.

Historically speaking, it can therefore no longer be denied that even the relatively recent law of celibacy is governed by the antiquated and ancient conviction that there is something unclean and slightly sinful about sexual intercourse (even in the context of sacramental marriage). This is not to deny that in the first ten centuries there were many priests who practised celibacy much more 'as monks', viz., for the sake of the kingdom of God (even Thomas makes a sharp distinction between the celibacy of the religious and that of the clergy 'because of considerations of purity').

Again historically, it seems to be of very secondary importance that other motives also played a role in the mediaeval law of celibacy; at all events, they do not seem to have exercised any demonstrable historical influence. For example, there was the mediaeval confiscation of the goods of 'priests' sons', through which the church fought itself clear of the tutelage of secular powers. In fact celibacy considerably increased the church's resources (and thus the independence of the church over against princes and emperors).[21] However, the ritual law of abstinence is the only decisive and the only determinative element in ecclesiastical legislation. It is therefore historically incorrect, and ideological, to regard the law of celibacy as a means used by the church to acquire power, at least in antiquity and in the Middle Ages. In later times, once the law was established, it began to function in the context of a struggle for power; but this has nothing to do with the reasons why it came into being.

It was only at the Second Vatican Council (at least in the canonical documents), for the first time in the whole of church history, that the traditional motivation for the law of celibacy was seen to have become untenable in modern times. For the first time, too, reference was made to Matt. 19.11f., so-called 'religious celibacy' for the sake of the kingdom of God, in connection with the celibacy of the ministry. Furthermore, this Council carefully avoided going over all the old reasons; it deliberately refrains from speaking of *perfecta castitas* (so as not to belittle those who are married), talking rather of *perfecta continentia*, in which context (though only because of strong pressure from Cardinal Bea) there is also praiseworthy commemoration of the non-celibate life-style of the priests of the Eastern church (something which the Council of Trent explicitly did not want).[22] Beyond question, since the Second Vatican Council the law of celibacy has been put on quite a different basis from that which it had in the earlier history of the church. In fact this presents the problem in a new way, though in this connection one cannot evade the problematical origin of this law. It must, however, be said that to lay open the history of the origin of a phenomenon does not imply anything either for or against its validity or truth. Methodologically speaking, these are two completely different questions. A reconstruction of the history of the origin of a phenomenon can, however, indicate the ideological elements involved in it.

On the other hand, it is impossible to say of a celibacy which has been voluntarily accepted, and experienced as a charisma, what one could justifiably say of the old law of abstinence, namely, that it goes back to an antiquated and mistaken anthropology. Although this raises another set of new problems (which I shall discuss below), it is impossible to dismiss celibacy (provided that there is no disdain for sexual or human relations), on the basis of religious or other noteworthy reasons (sometimes even fortuitous), with the slogan 'an antiquated anthropology'.

However, this does not solve all the problems. The new motivation for the celibacy of the ministry given by Vatican II also raises new questions. What is the precise meaning of 're-ligious celibacy', i.e. celibacy for the sake of the kingdom of God? This can have two meanings which, with some theological justification, for the sake of convenience I shall call 'mystical' and 'pastoral' (or apostolic), without being able to distinguish the two aspects adequately. The mystical and apostolic (and also the political) aspects are the two intrinsically connected aspects or dimensions of the one Christian life of faith. It is indeed justifiable and legitimate that someone should remain unmarried in order to be completely free for the service of church work and thus for his fellow human beings, just as others also do not marry (though that does not in fact imply 'celibacy') in order to devote themselves wholly to science, to art, to the struggle for a juster world, and so on. Sometimes it amounts to an existential feeling that no other course is possible. In other words, not to marry is seldom, if ever, the object of a person's real choice. The real object of the choice is 'something else', and this something else preoccupies some people to such an extent that they leave marriage on one side. Not marrying is usually not a choice in and of itself, but one 'for the sake of . . .': in religious terms, for the sake of the kingdom of God. As a result, we may not consider the negative and exclusive aspect of this choice, which is really for some other reason, in isolation and on its own. Of course in the life of any culture it so happens that a particular existential 'I cannot do otherwise' in the long run becomes ritualized. Thus, for example, the fact of 'not being able to eat' because of a death, or because, in a religious context, one is looking forward excitedly to the feast of the Passover, developed into a ritual: penitential fasting, or fasting for forty days. People then fast even though they may perhaps have a great longing to eat. We must not underestimate the ritualizing of life, though in every culture in the long run there is the threat of a formalized evacuation of the content of this ritualization. It becomes narrow and rigid, when it was originally meant to serve, or at least to evoke, an existential experience.

Thus although the theme of celibacy has become a pastoral and religious one, we must also be able to test the truth of the affirmation by the facts. Historically, it can be seen from the history of married leaders throughout the churches of the Reformation that in most cases the marriage of ministers has in no way hindered their utter dedication to the community; on the contrary, in many cases it has furthered this (in so far as we are able to judge on this question from a statistical investigation). One or the other depends purely on the person in question and cannot be established *a priori* in the abstract. The danger – and the facts – of egotism, unavailability and even boorishness on the part of celibates is not unknown, least of all among celibates themselves. Therefore the pastoral theme, even in its political dimension of the struggle for those who have been deprived of their rights, cannot become the decisive motive and argument for a universal law of celibacy. There remains, then, the 'mystical element' in celibacy for the sake of the kingdom of God, the service of mankind in the cause of the gospel, which can scarcely be distinguished from the 'pastoral element'.

Here the Second Vatican Council also introduced some important qualifications. Earlier, it was generally accepted that there was a kind of competition between love of God and married love, for reasons already given by Paul, namely, the need 'to please one's wife', which would detract from undivided love of God (I Cor. 7.32–34). This alleged competition, too, can no longer be justified theologically. For this reason Vatican II explicitly rejected a prepared text which said that 'undivided love' and 'dedication to God alone' must be seen as the real characteristics of religious celibacy. This competitive opposition between love of God and love of a fellow human being (including sexual love) was deliberately rejected. The definitive text runs: 'That precious gift of divine grace which the Father gives to some men . . . so that by virginity, or celibacy, they can more easily devote their entire selves to God alone with undivided heart' (*Lumen Gentium*, no. 42). It was thus conceded that total and undivided dedication to God is the calling of all Christians; according to this text from the Council, celibacy simply makes it to some degree 'easier' to realize this spirituality, which is in fact enjoined upon all Christians. If we purify the law of celibacy from all antiquated and incorrect motivation, which is what this Council wants to do, some basis in fact does remain, but it is a very narrow one, viz., an abstract and theoretical 'greater ease'. I call this 'abstract and theoretical': that is because in practice it can be easier for one person to arrive at a greater and more real and undivided love of God in marriage, whereas for someone else this only happens through an unmarried life. This, then, is the way in which the Tridentine view that unmarried life for the sake of the kingdom of God is a 'higher state' than the 'married state' has generally been interpreted in the theology of the last twenty years. The alleged superiority is dependent on the person in question, and cannot be established generally in purely abstract terms. What is better for one is less good and perhaps even oppressive for another, and vice versa. (In this connection a choice should be possible between 'a provisional celibacy in the service of the kingdom of God' and a celibacy intended to be 'perpetual', especially as in the course of a lifetime someone may arrive at the discovery that a perpetual celebacy undertaken as a convenience has in fact become a deep-rooted hindrance. However, we cannot discuss these problems here.)

If all this is correct, a universal law of celibacy for all ministers would at least be a serious exaggeration, on the basis of an abstraction, and therefore without concrete pastoral dimensions. At all events, one cannot interpret 'the new law', by which I mean the new motivation which Vatican II has given to the old law of celibacy, as a principle of selection, in the sense that the church chooses its ministers exclusively from Christians who voluntarily embrace celibacy. Given the earlier history of the existing law and the official custom of speaking of a law of celibacy,[23] despite new motivation, the canonical legislation persists in seeing the celibacy of the ministry as a kind of *statutory obligation* on the basis of an abstract and theoretical superiority of celibacy. Despite many affinities between ministry and celibacy, however, there are also unmistakable affinities between marriage and ministry, and the New Testament texts about 'the husband of one wife' point precisely in this direction.

However, many who argue for the detachment of priesthood from the ideal of celibacy do so primarily on the basis of an appeal to human rights. But anyone can in fact renounce his or her own rights (though not those of others)! Thus the question is whether here and there a liberal bourgeois conception of freedom does not sometimes take the place of gospel freedom. If – and this is clearly not the case, though since the Second Vatican Council it has increasingly become the practice from Rome – if voluntary celibacy is thus boosted as a principle of selection for the church's ministry, then in principle it is difficult to put forward decisive arguments against the 'celibacy of the ministry'. Any community has the right to impose principles of selection in the choice of its officials – in the case of the church, in the choice of its ministers. The New Testament also demonstrates this clearly (in the Pastoral Epistles). However, it must be conceded that this can often be the beginning of 'discrimination', though that need not necessarily be the case. Thus to my mind the only decisive argument for continuing to fight for the separation of ministry and celibacy (in other words, the only decisive argument against a law of celibacy) is twofold. On the one hand there is the credibility of the charisma of celibacy, freely chosen, in the eyes of the world and the person's own church (now, celibate priests are constantly under the suspicion of 'wanting to marry, but not being allowed to', as the common saying goes); on the other hand there is an argument from the theology of the church, viz., the right by grace for Christian communities to have presidents and to celebrate the eucharist. As a result of the present coupling of celibacy and ministry, at least in the Western church, in many places the apostolic vitality of the community and the celebration of the eucharist are endangered. In such a situation, church legislation, which can in any case be changed, must give way to the more urgent right to the apostolic and eucharistic building up of the community. (Finally, it is obvious that the pastoral authorities in the church must also, and above all, make a decision here.) However, one would be naive to think that the so-called 'crisis situation' among the clergy will be of short duration, or is even over. That is to underestimate the force of the old spirituality which made many young men accept celibacy because they in fact thought that marriage was indeed something of less value. This idealism, mistaken though it was, led many people in fact freely to accept the celibacy of the ministry. If marriage is given its full value (and it should be remembered that for Catholics, it is a sacrament), the vocations to a religious celibate life will of course decrease. One could say: earlier, people in fact chose not to marry because marriage was a lesser, indeed almost a mistaken 'good'. In that case celibacy can directly be an object of choice.

Nowadays a direct choice of celibacy (apart from the real choice of some other good which proves utterly demanding) is in fact ambivalent. Often it is even suspect.

At this point I should also indicate the 'ideological element' that can be present in an appeal to 'prayer for vocation'. No Christian would deny the value and the force of prayer, even for vocations; but if the reason for the shortage of priests is 'church legislation' which can be changed and modified in the course of time for pastoral reasons, then a call to prayer can act as an excuse; in other words, it can be a reason for not changing this law.

(b) The so-called 'third way'

Finally, even after everything that the Second Vatican Council has said on the subject, the precise content of the official church view of celibacy as such still remains obscure and vague. This emerges from a new set of questions which (at least in their modern form and the practice to which they give rise) only arose after this council. Here I am referring to the problem of the so-called 'third way', at least understood as 'shared celibacy' (and including abstinence). From the whole of the earlier legislation of the church it is clear that the church has never pronounced against the love of a priest (although not married) for someone else (in fact a woman is meant). The church has always condemned exclusively genital sexuality, and what leads to that. This is evident even from the Second Lateran Council, in which the law of celibacy was formulated for the first time: the legal prohibition of marriage was only intended to safeguard observation of the law of abstinence more effectively.

With the Second Vatican Council, which wanted to exclude any disparagement of sexuality, the situation is to some extent different, although a certain ambiguity remains. The basic reason for religious celibacy is now in fact the 'greater ease' for universal, Christian undivided love of God, though this greater ease is given specific form as 'complete abstinence'. In other words, in essence, down to Vatican II the law of celibacy essentially remains a law of abstinence. Here a connection is established between complete abstinence and an easier undivided love of God, but not with presence or absence of the love of a woman, which does not arise. The over-riding concern is the exclusion of sexuality, and not love. And in that case the urgent question arises whether the motivation of this Council is anthropologically so essentially different from the earlier motivation. Here we come to the real heart of the problem of celibacy in a modern context, a problem on which ecclesiastical legislation has still never pronounced – except in the Synod of Dutch Bishops at Rome in January 1980. (Here it remains uncertain precisely what the synod understood by 'the third way': what does one mean by a middle way 'between marriage and celibacy'?) If we interpret this Synod along the lines of 'shared celibacy' (with a view to complete abstinence), then for the first time in the history of the church, or at least in the church's legislation, we have a pronouncement which is completely new, viz., that it is of the nature of celibacy to exclude not only sexuality but also 'the love of a woman'. It would certainly be extreme for one 'particular synod' to make a decision on the nature of the charisma of celibacy which differed radically from anything that had happened before in church history! It is at all events impossible to appeal to Vatican II in connection with the Synod's decision (interpreted in the sense mentioned above).

The problem itself is by no means new in the literature of Christian spirituality. On the contrary. But it is completely new in the canonical legislation of the Catholic church (which is what I am concerned with now). Here the real problems connected with 'celibacy as such' are formulated in the most profound way . . . and left unanswered. At all events, what does the mystical and pastoral element of religious celibacy involve? What is at stake is the anthropologically inner relationship between sexuality and love. And precisely this anthropological question is left unanswered throughout the legislation of the church. This confronts us with a new dilemma. Either we are dealing purely with a law of abstinence, in which case the question is: does 'physical abstinence' as such, of itself, ever have a religious value? That is hard to affirm if we do not want to fall back into the old attitude which is opposed to sexuality. Or it is a matter of a degree of competition between love for God and love for a fellow human being – let me limit it here to love of a woman. And this, too, is theologically unjustifiable. However, it is impossible, anthropologically, to separate the two problems unless one wants to dehumanize sexuality and make it a purely physical phenomenon.

Thus the subject under discussion is either a competing love or a physical act. The one is theologically unjustifiable and the other is anthropologically unjustifiable. It is obvious that here we need renewed study of, and reflection on, human sexuality if we are to acquire a clearer understanding of the nature of 'religious celibacy'.

Within this short space, at any rate, I want merely to point to a first attempt in this direction made above all by J. Pohier, who on the one hand is opposed to the anti-sexual views of antiquated anthropology and on the other has made a psychological analysis of the 'ambiguity' of all sexuality.[24] Sexuality is indeed a two-edged sword which can also evoke dark powers. Over-sexualized society and the misuse of sexuality in our culture are the clearest indication of this. Sex has become a consumer article and a means to power. Precisely here religious celibacy can in fact function as an acute criticism of humanity and society, to the benefit of truly human sexuality and to the advantage of mankind itself. As abstinence, it is a religious protest both against 'liberalism' and against all forms of subjugation and 'objectification'. A certain trend in feminism bears witness to this. However, such abstinence does not tell against sexuality as such in any way whatsoever; still less does it tell against human love, which never competes with love of God.

However, it cannot be demonstrated *a priori* whether, anthropologically speaking, despite human weakness, such deeper love represented by a 'celibate protest' can, through complete abstinence, finally be turned into a realistic and truly human possibility. Experiments which at the moment are being carried on all over the world will eventually give us better information about this. Here naivety is not the best teacher, far less anxiety and strictness! Nevertheless, in my view the debate about celibacy is not closed; it has barely been opened. And that is where I will leave the question for the moment.

(c) Women in the ministry

In connection with all this, something must also be said about women in the ministry. The church's resistance to this is very closely connected with the way in which the ritual laws of purity led to the celibacy of males.

In 1976 the Congregation for the Doctrine of the Faith produced a declaration on the question of women in the ministry.[25] The fact that this was not a *motu proprio* from the Pope but a document produced by a Congregation, albeit with the approval of the Pope, indicates a certain hesitation on the part of the Pope to make a 'definitive' pronouncement on the question; this is the Roman way of keeping a matter open, though provisionally a kind of 'magisterial statement' on the issue has been made. According to its own words, this document sets out to make a contribution to the struggle for women's liberation.

However, as long as women are left completely outside all decision-making authorities in the church, there can be no question of real women's liberation. Nevertheless, this document says that women are excluded from leadership in the church on grounds of their sex, because they are excluded from presiding at the eucharist. Here, in a pre-conciliar way, the connection between church and ministry is again broken in favour of the relationship between eucharist (sacred power) and ministry. In particular, all kinds of feminine 'impurities' have unmistakably played a part throughout the history of the church in restricting women's role in worship, as also in the Levitical legislation and in many cultures. What were originally hygienic measures are later 'ritualized'. All this is in no way specifically Christian.

But why must the fact that, given the culture of the time, Jesus only chose twelve men as apostles, suddenly acquire a theological significance, while at the same time the similar fact that this same Jesus for the most part (perhaps even entirely) chose only married men for this task, along with the fact that Paul demands the apostolic right to involve his own wife in the apostolic work (I Cor. 9.5; though Paul renounces his own claim to this right), is not allowed any theological significance, and moreover is interpreted in the opposite direction through the law of celibacy? Two standards are used, depending on the particular interest. This mutually conflicting, arbitrarily selective biblical hermeneutic (or method of interpretation) shows that here non-theological themes unconsciously play a decisive role, while being presented on the authority of the Bible. (I am reluctant to express this sharp criticism, but honesty compels me to speak out.) As a Catholic theologian I know that magisterial pronouncements can be correct even when the arguments used in them are unsound. But in that case something meaningful must be said somewhere about the exclusion of women from the ministry. That is not the case here, and all the arguments tend, rather, to converge on the insight that this is a purely historically conditioned cultural pattern, understandable in antiquity and even until recently, but problematical in a changed culture which is aware of real discrimination against women. All the arguments in favour of 'another attractive task' for women in the church, on the basis of 'her own feminine' characteristics and intuitions, may sound fine, but they do not provide any support for the exclusion of women from leadership in the church. On the contrary. Of course we must allow on the other hand that the church authorities must not take any over-hasty steps here while their own church people (does sociology support this view?) are perhaps still some way from this awareness; however, this is quite different from looking round rather desperately for arguments which do not seem able to stand up to any criticism and are simply concerned to legitimate the *status quo*.

I would like to illustrate the morass into which these two interconnected questions – celibacy in the ministry and the woman's role in the ministry – can bog down the vital gospel of many churches by a *cri de coeur* which comes from an African church. It asked that its married 'mokambi' or lay catechist, who for years had been a successful leader of a Christian community in Zaire, should be consecrated priest: 'Dear Cardinal Maloela, our community has a mokambi, a gifted leader of our community. But he is not allowed to preside at the eucharist . . .' [26] Cardinal Maloela, himself long convinced that there were obstacles in the church, could only answer: 'Is this not a challenge from the Holy Spirit, a sign of the times which compels us to look for other ways than those on which we in our church are bent?' [27] Thus the hindrances in the case of both priestly celibacy and women in the ministry seem to me at root to be of a pseudo-doctrinal kind, and are to be found especially in the ontological and sacerdotalist conception of the ministry in the setting of worship in the Western Latin church. In many religions and, in ancient times, even in the Christian church, for once to put it bluntly, 'taboos' were associated with this sacralism: both feminine and sexual taboos.

(d) A charisma is not to be used as a 'political ploy'

On the other hand, the church-political pressure which in some cases is exercised on those who offer themselves for the priesthood and who voluntarily accept celibacy, seems to me to be equally unjustified. So long as the present church order remains in force, a plea for the separation of the compulsory connection between ministry and celibacy, also with a view to the possibility that the charisma of celibacy, freely accepted, may gain in credibility, must not be the occasion for dissuading those who are in the grasp of this charisma, on the ground that to remain celibate can only strengthen the existing church order. This last point may indeed be true; the pressure from church politics does not seem to me to be exercised from pure motives; it is wrong to use a charisma for political ends. Put in theoretical scientific terms, this means that the political efficacy of an insight may never come to replace its theoretical force. I therefore disapprove of this pressure which is clearly evident here and there. It makes no sense to state verbally that in addition to the ministry for those who are married there is also a special task for those who freely accept celibacy in the ministry, if one deters those who want to embark upon this venture. Of course, in view of what we have learnt through the humane sciences and a great many experiences, we have to concede that voluntary 'celibacy for mystical and political reasons' is not granted to the majority, not even to all ministers. Furthermore, at this point we must also think of those who for other than 'directly apostolic' reasons (many of which can be quite respectable, including, for example, homosexuality), remain unmarried and at the same time can be called to the ministry.

In conclusion (in connection with these and other contemporary problems connected with the ministry) it is my view that we cannot simply put all the blame on 'Rome'. Leadership or authority can only be exercised meaningfully and bring about change if it is successful in shaping the consciousness of both the community of believers and its ministers, including the bishops. It is impossible to ask the highest authority in the world church to alter church order if this change is not going to meet with the approval of the majority of Christian communities. This would be the beginning of a massive schism, which would then have to be healed again ecumenically some twenty years later (see the division in the Episcopal Church in America after the introduction of the ordination of women). In the meantime we have become wiser as a result of earlier schisms.

Consequently I see the phenomenon of the grass roots communities, specifically with their critical attitude, as in fact a ferment in a general moulding of consciousness; a stimulus to the official church and thus also a provisional and in fact necessary 'exception', albeit within the one great alliance of apostolic churches. This is an often marginal position through which consciousness is constantly stimulated, so that the great church becomes ripe for the introduction of another and better pastoral church order which in our time will give a modern form to the apostolicity of the Christian community.

V

A Brief Hermeneutical Intermezzo

In this short chapter I want to introduce a few reflections in order to forestall possible objections which could be made to the perspectives I shall present on the future (Chapter VI).

1. Someone might object to everything that has been said so far (and in fact to the whole of this book): have you not read history with an eye to the present problems associated with the ministry?

My answer is, 'Of course'. But at the same time I deny what is suggested here. That is the only way in which history can be read. Even the person who claims to read old documents in a 'neutral' way cannot think away his own present; he is wrong if he thinks that he can. In that case he is simply not aware of his own hidden interests. Whether consciously or unconsciously, people look at historical documents in the light of present-day questions, suppositions and hypotheses. The critical problem is whether one simply looks to history to confirm one's own already established views or whether one allows them to be put to the test by history.

Anyone who reads a book which was perhaps written two thousand years ago is himself addressed by the book; in that case he reads it in the light of his own questions and hypotheses, whether or not he is aware of the fact. Only a 'dogmatic' reader reads into the past what happens in his own street. Today's questions, formulated consciously and openly, are quite different from disguised prejudices; they are the necessary, albeit inadequate, prerequisite of being able to read old texts with an eye to their own significance for us now. The past is not a computer from which stored information can constantly be drawn afresh. That view is historicism, a wrong view of history. On the other hand, the reader must allow the texts to be 'texts'; in other words, recognize their own consistency. This is the only way in which he can get an answer from the texts to present-day questions, even if it is an indirect one, an answer which by understanding sense at the same time creates sense. We need creative trust in the text, without anticipating 'dogmatically' what its meaning is for us. It is a matter of beginning from contemporary questions and allowing ourselves to be addressed by the texts from within their own structure. Present and past now form a dialectical process, for the simple reason that we readers are part of the same human history as that in which the texts were written. The story began long before we start to take up its threat. Someone once said that the last thing that a fish (after achieving reflective awareness) would observe would be the water in which it lived: the 'today' of its own milieu. This is so familiar and obvious that it never strikes us. Thus everyone spontaneously reads the past through the prism of the present, his or her own present with its particular questions, presuppositions and hypotheses. To read a text critically and thus 'objectively' (in accordance with the material in question) is therefore also to be aware of all this; the uncritical readers of texts are those who want to read it 'unhistorically', and claim that they can exclude their own present in reading it.

Anyone who is unfamiliar with this hermeneutical structure of our historical human awareness begins to look at the past 'scientistically', i.e. ideologically, because in that case contemporary views are often legitimated unconsciously by reading the text, because they play an uncontrolled role in that reading.

Thus the practice of particular Christian, and above all critical, communities was the stimulus and the challenge to this study. Does this mean that the actual alternative practices of these Christian communities and their leaders in relation to the ministry become the 'norm and truth', and thus determine the reading of earlier texts? Not at all: that would be pure empiricism or pragmatism. Even pastoral effectiveness is not decisive in matters of truth; in this sense I reject the so-called principle of 'orthopraxis' as a principle of truth. (In that case the 'orthopraxis' of a thorough-going Nazi would also validate the 'orthodoxy' of Nazism as truth! I.e., thorough-going belief in a doctrine does not of itself make that doctrine true or sound.) The actual practice of Christian communities, legally or illegally, depending on the norms of canonical church order, is the *interpretandum*, i.e. what must be justified in theory, and must perhaps be criticized. For a theologian, what is called Christian practice is never a direct norm, but his agenda, i.e. that which he must clarify *secundum scripturas*, in the light of the great Christian tradition. On its side, practice must never wait for the permission of theologians before it gets going. That is certainly true. Whether justifiably or not, practice follows from faith (i.e. the spontaneous or implicit 'theory'), and so practice does not precede faith, but theology. However, the theologian must make a reflective investigation of the 'spontaneity' of this practice of faith, because this spontaneity can unconsciously admit uncritical elements and even allow a particular practice to prevail because it is supposed to be the 'practice of faith'. The theoretical justification of the theologian can also demonstrate by a reference to scripture and tradition, with a practical and critical end in view, whether the practice is in fact the expression of the movement of the Holy Spirit or rather that of the whims of personal preference. A successful justification demonstrates whether what is in fact happening (seen from a global perspective) is directed by the Holy Spirit. Thus the theologian turns into theory, in a critical way, what is presented in the effective practice of Christian communities and their leaders today as a concrete solution to urgent pastoral needs. So by nature the theologian is always the 'latecomer' in respect of Christian practice, which precedes him. But in his own time this latecomer is extremely necessary and irreplaceable, especially when it comes to demonstrating in a rational way whether this practice is *secundum scripturas*. An intuitive certainty here is not enough, and could open up the way to all kinds of arbitrariness. To the theologian, the actual practice of Christians and Christian communities is for the time being simply a possible sign of faith; he investigates whether it is a real sign of faith. This secondary but necessary demand for theological reflection thus clearly presupposes the practice of the community. But no practice of any kind is legitimated solely by itself. Only theological theory can demonstrate whether the direction of the practice is *orthos*, right (*orthopraxis*), in the light of the inspiration and orientation of the great Christian tradition, even if this practice should be completely new. You do not change the world or the church by 'ideas', and to change the world or the church is not of itself salvation, truth or happiness. *What* are the changes? That is the critical question. In a theological justification of them the theologian plays an irreplaceable role, unless practice is to become a runaway horse. We are therefore concerned with what I said above was the 'logos' or Christian reason of practice. But once this is assured, the practice of the Christian community is in fact the sphere in which theology is born and theory is at the same time a function of practice. However, we would have an ideology if theology were put directly – i.e. without the mediation of hermeneutics and in accordance with its own laws, laws in this sense independent of all practice – at the service of practice, whether that of the grass-roots communities or of the church authorities. That would theoretically amount to opportunism.

2. In this connection the problem of Christian obedience in faith and 'loyal opposition' is also relevant.

Today Christians have become more clearly aware that 'the will of God' is known to us only through the medium of history. There are dangerous ways of talking about 'the will of God'. If this will is known to us only through the medium of experiences in the world and in the church, and also through directives from the pastoral authority of the church, this means that we are never confronted unambiguously with the will of God; we trust that we are fulfilling the will of God.

Furthermore, ethics is a different language-game from the language of religion or belief. Religion is not just ethics and cannot be reduced to ethics, though on the other hand there is an intrinsic connection between religion and ethics. An understanding of the difference between good and evil is logically prior to the understanding of God and his will. This means that we do not define our moral obligations as human beings in the first instance in terms and concepts of 'God's will', but in terms of what tends towards worth and happiness in human life. On the other hand, a believer can and may rightly interpret what he sees here and now to be an urgent human need as an expression of the will of God without forfeiting the seriousness of God's will or reducing God in a bourgeois way to a merely eschatological judge of the use of human autonomy.

Precisely these historical mediations of God's will introduce a dialectic into Christian obedience. In this sense, from a Christian point of view in some instances illegality is a higher form of trust in the spirit of God; at all events it is also a trust in God which cannot be reduced to obedience to the authority of the church. Christian obedience is also listening, so as to be involved in the *kairos* or the moment of grace at a particular time, listening in obedience to the suffering of human beings and the seeds of a Christian community, and then performing specific actions in conformity to this 'voice of God'. This is also and above all a fundamental form of Christian obedience, derived from the authority of human beings who are suffering and in need. Thus a conflict can in fact arise between obedience to the will of God as mediated through events in the world and the church, and the will of God as mediated through the authority of the church. The conflict does not arise from the will of God as such, but is caused by the *intermediaries* which give divergent interpretations of it. In such a conflict Thomas Aquinas allows a man's conscience which has been tested in such a conflict (not just because it is sure of itself) to make the decision and moreover adds that the conscientious person must do this 'even if he knows that as a result he can be excommunicated by the church'. In my view this applies above all whenever the salvation and happiness of others are at stake (because one can always renounce one's own rights for the sake of something better). This is in no way to minimize church authority; it simply means that Christian obedience is not to be reduced to obedience to the mediation of God's will through the church. In addition there is also Christian obedience to 'the signs of the time' as God's *kairos* for humankind, though we ourselves must decipher these signs.

VI

Some Perspectives on the Future: Contextual Experience of Ministry within a Living Community

The future of church communities and ministry within them is determined not only by the community of the church but also by the church's official leadership. After the first breakthrough at the Second Vatican Council, at a Synod of Bishops in 1971 the church began to reflect on what is called 'the crisis in the priesthood'. Consequently, an analysis of this synod fits into the framework of the present book, not least for one particular reason. At this synod it became evident that the majority of Catholic bishops throughout the world are open to a new practice in the ministry, while on the other hand the official organs of the church are a serious hindrance to these desires and new visions.

1. Forgotten events: the 1971 Synod of Bishops on the ministry. Between Vatican II and 1980

(a) An analysis of speeches in the debate

In the period after the Second Vatican Council, the process begun in the Council began to go further, both at the level of exegetical and dogmatic studies and also at the level of the living practice of church communities.

From both sides it has become clear that a more empirical approach to the problem of the ministry and the practice of official ministry has begun to prevail in the church. This has wrongly, but understandably, given the impression that the pneuma-christological character of the ministry is on the way out and that ministry is seen purely as delegation by the community, without further theological implications. Although this sociological 'professionalization' may be the intention here and there, i.e. that the priest should ultimately be seen as a kind of social worker, this is by no means the basic tenor of these new practical and theoretical approaches, whether among theologians or among priests. Although it was largely based on a misunderstanding, or to a small degree on one or two disparaging interpretations of the ministry, a reaction began to develop. In turn, others spoke more strongly about the ministry in supernaturalistic terms than before. A certain polarization became inevitable. It is against this background of two powerful extremes, 'supernaturalism' (and 'fideism') on the one hand, and 'horizontalism' on the other, that we need to see the second 'ordinary synod' of October 1971.[1] This synod did not propose any kind of solution, because it still thought ecclesiologically in a dualistic way and therefore could not provide any meaningful correction on the one hand to supernaturalist conceptions and on the other to conceptions which saw the ministry simply as a profession and which did not express its real religious depth, or passed it over.

Even before the synod, the conferences of bishops could inform Rome about their reactions to the synod working paper which was sent to all the bishops. A résumé of these reactions was sent to members of the synod by the synod secretariat. Here the sense of all the bishops that their priests were caught up in a crisis of identity came clearly to the fore. In addition, on the basis of these written reactions from bishops, Bishop Enrico Bartoletti, Apostolic Administrator of Lucca, gave a panoramic survey of present problems connected with the priesthood, at the beginning of the synod debate. Of course this survey, with both positive and negative aspects, was incomplete, and was not always clear and accurate in its analysis or explanations; generally speaking, however, it gave an adequate background against which the synod could reflect on the pastoral demands of the moment. Nevertheless, factors within the church causing disquiet to priests were played down, and in a somewhat supernaturalistic way the survey pointed out that priests have virtually stopped praying and are one-sidedly involved in social and political affairs. No analysis was made of the so-called loss of a sense of transcendence, so that the survey gave the impression that, given a revival of prayer, all could be well again. This unmistakably carried with it the connotation that no alterations to the *status quo* in the church were necessary. It is here that we find the supernaturalism of this attitude. Furthermore, it made the call to prayer lose credibility.

This approach to the problem of the priesthood was expressed in harsher terms in the actual synod working paper, so that its positive aspects were robbed of all credibility by the issues that were not mentioned in it. After the general speeches in the plenary sessions, the bishops were also given topics to discuss in the *circuli minores*, i.e. the twelve discussion groups in which the bishops could take part, depending on the language that they could speak. These topics were determined by the agenda of the synod and the speeches given in the debate. The groups' answers on the topics were to provide the basic material for the definitive version of the synod's view of the priestly ministry.

By way of a survey, I shall sum up the points discussed, from both the doctrinal and the pastoral (the official term was 'practical') parts of the synod working paper. This survey already gives a direct perspective on the actual course of the synod, for which it would finally decide.

The key points in the doctrinal section were questions over which doubts had arisen in the minds of many priests. These were: the specificity or the 'distinctiveness' of the official priesthood as compared with the universal priesthood of believers; a more than purely functional conception of the church's ministry; and the ministry as a representation of the one priesthood of Christ over against the Christian community (there was a clear tendency to focus this contrast on the priest as the official president at the celebration of the eucharist, as happened at the Council of Trent). There was also a concern not to suggest any opposition between purely charismatic churches and churches with an official organization. However, the ministry of the church must nevertheless be seen within the whole context of the one mission of the entire church for ministry: the official ministry is a specific form of this mission. The ministry does not come 'from below', but 'from above', just as salvation itself is given to us from above. In other words, a position is adopted here against those who would claim – and this is the way in which 'from below' is interpreted – that the ministry of the church is 'purely a social ministry of leadership by way of a mandate from the community' (*Relatio* by Cardinal Höffner, 5 October 1971).

Along with Cardinal Höffner's second *Relatio* (from which the key points quoted above have been taken), another list of six key points was sent through the secretariat of the synod. These had been compiled on behalf of the synod by the International Theological Commission.[2] There was also a list with eight key points which had come from the conference of German bishops. By and large these three lists were concerned with the same problems, though the accents were different. Nevertheless, the discussion groups were left free to do as they liked with these 'prefabricated resolutions', since officially the question put to the discussion groups was: 'In your view, what are the key doctrinal questions on which the synod must pronounce in its major proposals?' (*Relatio* of Cardinal Höffner). The individual points here were: some doubt about the priestly character, and priesthood 'for a specific period'; doubt about the direct institution of the presbyterate by Christ; the opposition seen by some between Trent and Vatican II; and, once more and most emphatically, the connection and the difference between the priesthood of the community (the universal priesthood) and the official priesthood. (Shortly before the synod the International Theological Commission met again to study these doubts, which were also evident from the written reactions of the bishops to the agenda of the synod).

Although the 'Report on the Priesthood' by the Pastoral Council of the Netherlands need not necessarily have been in mind, it is nevertheless clear that all the problems posed there are directly connected with the key points indicated in the synod and presented to the synod. It is evident from the speeches at the debate that the Dutch approach was not just typical of Holland, but reflects a world-wide view of many bishops, priests and theologians.

Seven clear questions were presented as points for discussion in connection with the second, pastoral section, and the discussion groups had to give answers to them. 1. What is the relationship between the evangelizing activities of the priest (preaching, catechetics and building up the community, or: the work of formation, welfare and development, etc.), and his liturgical and sacramental, i.e. sacral activity? What is the relationship between the activities of the priest as minister and the secular calling or 'temporary job' which may well be carried on by the priest? What is the shared responsibility of the priest in the whole of the pastoral undertaking, given on the one hand priestly participation in the concerns of the bishop and on the other participation by the whole of the local church? In connection with the celibacy of the priesthood: on the one hand there is the matter of the preservation of the discipline of celibacy in the Latin church; on the other hand, what is to be said about the desirability of ordaining priests those who are already married? 5. What should be the spiritual life of the priest? 6. What financial provisions need to be made to arrive at a fairer remuneration for all priests (within a diocese, a province of the church, or the world church)? 7. What guidelines can be given for training for the priesthood and for post-ordination training and continued education? This was the whole complex of issues on which the synod had to make some meaningful pronouncement. To whom? To the Pope? Or directly to the priests? This question was never answered. However, if one is saying anything, it is vitally important to know to whom one is saying it.

First of all, it should be pointed out that some bishops were unhappy about the division between doctrinal and pastoral sections. The French bishops, in particular, pointed out that this division is disastrous, and that one can only make a pastoral approach to the church's ministry in modern times, in fidelity to the gospel and the apostolic tradition, on the basis of contemporary 'signs of the times', i.e. the specific questions and problems raised by priests, and by reflecting on what they do. Furthermore, this seems to be to be a hermeneutical necessity: one cannot give an *a priori* definition of what a priest needs to be 'in himself'; his relationship to the present is part of the very nature of priesthood. Here the past is necessary, as a warning to remind us that we should not have a blind fixation on the present. Human life is the place where the past defines and opens up the possibilities of the future. The synod did not discover the art of listening to the past as the question which the future puts to us now, in circumstances which are different from the past. On the other hand, without a decision for the present, remembrance of the past remains a repetition of how priests in their time (our past) have been devoted to the gospel: it does not call for an encounter with the needs of the present. Because of our repetition of old traditions, we do not seem to be in a position to produce new ones, as happened as a result of the activity of the past. Without the experiment of historical experience, neither we nor a synod can tell what ought to be the significance of the church's ministry in our own time.

However, the majority of the members of the synod resorted to the 'deductive method': they began from doctrinal positions in the past in their attempt to find a practical solution for today. Of course they were all agreed that in the last resort a synod does not need to do what a Council does; indeed, this is impossible. In fact it was resolved that because of 'the uncertainty of younger men as a result of contemporary theological ideas' (*Relatio* of Cardinal Höffner), the synod needed to establish, with some force, a number of unassailable principles for the priesthood. These were to be expressed in quite short basic statements. Because the task was expressed in this way, there was every chance that the twelve groups would begin their discussions in a conservative or even reactionary atmosphere. For when priests embark on experiments, in the first stages of course there is always chaff with the corn. But when there is a tendency towards conservatism, the accent tends to lie on the shadow side of the experiment and not on those insights within it which provide hope for the church. Mgr Ramon Echarren Isturriz, auxiliary bishop of Madrid, had already seen this clearly when he remarked in a speech during the debate: 'The ways of faith are always and necessarily ways of creativity. . . We should keep firmly before our eyes the fact that the present crisis in the priesthood cannot be solved only through this theology, which itself partially bears the guilt for the crisis.'[3] This Spaniard said that earlier theology was one of the causes of the crisis of identity among priests. On the other hand, however, Bishop Anthony Padiyara of Kerala was a spokesman for precisely the opposite point of view. 'The present crisis, I am afraid, is in part at least due to the unrestrained activity of those theological writers who come out with dogmatic pronouncements with scant regard for the Magisterium and the age-long ecclesiastical tradition. In some of their statements one hardly notices a reverence for the sacred or a sense of faith.' The polarization or hardening of the different views which arise within the church was reflected in the synod. Diametrically opposed statements could be heard in the debate. Just a few examples, taken from many, should be enough. On the one hand: there is a clear tendency among our priests to engage in purely social and political questions on the pretext of preaching the gospel (Bishop R. F. Primatesta, Argentina); on the other hand: 'The crisis among priests lies in the fact that they cannot recognize the integration of the human and social liberation movement in the gospel' (Bishop E. Pironio, Argentina). On the one hand: 'Sociology and psychology have taken the place of grace and prayer, and in place of profound purity there comes the pseudo-scientific impurity of psychoanalysis' (Cardinal A. dell'Acqua, in a speech greeted with applause, reading out a passage from a letter written by a teacher in an Italian grammar school); on the other hand, many speeches from bishops criticized the agenda of the synod because it spoke disparagingly and negatively about the contribution of the humane sciences in pastoral approaches to the problem of the priesthood. On the one hand: 'Are not we bishops also responsible for the crisis of identity experienced by our priests?' (Bishop A. Lorscheider, Brazil; Cardinal Alfrink); on the other hand: ar-

guments put forward by priests make it impossible to fulfil the
role of a bishop (Bishop A. Baroni, Sudan). On the one hand:
one individual criticized Pope Paul VI, with a reference to Canon 131 par. 1 and Canon 1072, for wanting to give too many
dispensations to priests who wanted to marry (Bishop Y. Ijjas,
Hungary), while on the other hand: one person (in passing)
criticized the Pope for calling priests who marry 'apostates and
faithless' (*inter alia*, the Superior General of the White Fathers,
P. T. van Asten), instead of regarding them, with love and
righteousness, at least as completely integrated members of the
Christian community (the Canadian and French bishops, and
a number of others); it was important for everyone to make a
personal study of how far these priests could again be involved
in some pastoral work on the grounds of their earlier priestly
experience (above all the Canadian bishops).

This short survey may be enough to indicate the polarization
in the synod. Its consequences for the final proposals of the
synod were far-reaching, at least given that the synod, which
in accordance with domestic rules offers advice to the Pope,
was intrinsically inclined to arrive at as much unanimity as
possible. That in fact seemed to be the purpose. An advisory
resolution from the synod carries so much moral weight in
public that although the Pope can in fact dissociate himself from
it, it is not easy for him to do so. A large degree of unanimity
of course makes it easier for the Pope to show his approval of
the decision of a synod. However, given the existing polarization, the result of this mechanism was that it was only possible
to arrive at a degree of unanimity at the cost of failing to make
courageous pastoral decisions. As a result, from an institutional
point of view the synod was, of course, inconclusive, a lowest
common denominator which on one point – *mirabile dictu* – at
least in the discussion groups proved even more minimalist
than the Pope himself (reluctantly, but with justification) had
felt to be possible in principle (in his letter of February 1970 to
Cardinal Villot). Thus this synod became more Roman than the
Pope.

The synod was unable to achieve its goal, that of reaching
unanimity at least in a central, uniform perspective, i.e. of
attempting to give a universal, uniform answer to problems
which presented themselves in quite different ways in the different local churches. A very different possibility, namely that,
given the great local differences and the polarization and conflicting opinions, a unanimous decision could have been made
to recognize the pastoral competence of local churches, with

their conferences of bishops, as being the most urgent pastoral need of our time, was raised only by a minority at the synod.[4] This, regardless of the fact that in the previous, extraordinary synod the way had been opened for the possibility of a pluri-form solution and for an adaptation of the principle of subsi-diarity to the pastoral sphere. At any rate, this synod said more hopeful things about the local church than had emerged from Vatican II. Furthermore, this pastoral possibility is theologically justified on the basis of the consecration which in principle gives the bishop all necessary authority for the pastoral support of the community which is in fact entrusted to him. The only limitation that can be placed on this authority is the need for collegial solidarity with the welfare of the whole church. (While this idea is correct in itself, it must not lead to the victimization of particular local churches in favour of an abstract 'general well-being'). The fact that the synod was not brave enough to take account of this possibility may perhaps be described in subsequent history as the 'great refusal' which explains its fail-ure. Perhaps Bishop Damert Bellido (Peru) felt this when in a speech in a debate on the priesthood he said, 'Any attempt at changing an infrastructure (in this case the priesthood) within a greater structure (the church) without changing this greater structure is a utopia':[5] he could have said, putting it more precisely, 'an ideology'. This statement did not attract any at-tention either in the debate or in the press, but the speaker hit the nail on the head and at the same time condemned in an-ticipation the dubious outcome of the synod. Thus R. Weak-land, Abbas Primus of the Benedictine Confederation, already seemed to be too late with his appeal finally to stop any attempt at *aggiornamento* and instead of adapting the church to the world, now to take 'the lead' as the church and adopt a critical attitude to the world.[6] The synod had already resolved in fact not even to continue Pope John's programme of *aggiornamento*, and as an institution was doomed to pre-conciliar conservatism. Let me make this clearer by highlighting some other points from the synod.

It is significant that some conservatively-minded representa-tives found even the synod working paper too modern and theologically unsound. They referred to the Council of Trent to demonstrate that this agenda did not adequately express the ontological, sacral character of the priesthood. The consequence of this ontological interest was a call for an exact definition of the 'essential difference' (Vatican II) between the universal priesthood and the official priesthood. This interest became almost an obsession with many bishops, above all when it seemed that other members of the synod thought that a functional distinction was enough to underline the view of Vatican II. The fact that this functional distinction was denied here and there in some critical grass-roots communities, in theory or in practice, made some bishops take refuge, out of fright, in preconciliar conceptions. The general result of this was a return to the one-sided approach of the Council of Trent, understandable at that time, which ultimately associates the distinctive character of the official priesthood almost exclusively with the eucharist and the hearing of confessions. Thus the wider perspective in which Vatican II had seen the priesthood was completely abandoned.

Despite this narrowing, one cannot miss a complete shift in the problem of the priesthood at the synod, as compared with Vatican II. The Second Vatican Council was concerned with a revaluation of the priest primarily as one who preaches the word and, as leader, provides a stimulus, or is the pioneer who builds up the community. This contrasts with Trent's exclusive accent on the sacral, i.e. sacramental, cultic activity of the priest. In the synod, on the other hand, the activity of the church (proclamation and the formation and leadership of the community, along with the ministry of the sacraments), is called the sacral activity of the priest, but now in contrast to the social and political involvement of the priest, and also in contrast to his possible secular profession. The context of the synod is of course quite different from that of Vatican II and is a reflection of developments in the exercising of the priesthood, above all in critical and grass-roots communities, and by many individual priests.

In fact this new practice among priests dominated all the debates on the priesthood in the synod, whether or not this was expressly stated. Among some bishops a clear understanding of these new accents can be detected; among the others, in reaction to 'refractory priests, globe-trotting theologians and the communication media' – according to some bishops the three causes of the crisis over the priesthood – a clearly conservative, pre-conciliar tendency can be detected. For many bishops the actual situation of priests today therefore makes the question of the essential difference between priest and laity the key issue at the synod, while the New Testament obviously is little concerned with drawing any clear dividing lines, though it recognizes the particularity of each member's charisma and service. In fact many members of the synod wanted an *a priori* definition, a sharp delimitation, so that they could solve all problems with a convenient rule of thumb: the problem of political involvement, the question of secular professions, the problem of celibacy and so on.

Anyone who makes a careful study of the tone of the speeches in the debates will sense that the same group of problems lurks everywhere: fear of identifying the message of the gospel with social and political, critical and even revolutionary trends towards liberation. There is a fear of connecting Christian identity with human integrity and liberation. In fact to reduce the gospel and the liberation of purely Christian salvation to the problem of changing social and political structures is an unmistakable temptation of our time. However, anxiety-reactions are seldom healthy, and threaten to form an excuse for ignoring the evident need for these changes. It is in fact difficult to divide the two problems of the synod – priesthood and righteousness in the world – in the minds of its members. So if no meaningful pastoral approach could be achieved to either the first or the second group of problems, one could hardly expect a meaningful conclusion to both of them. Bishops who do not want to give up the social *status quo* in their country argue for an apolitical church, and oppose the active politicization of the task of the priest. On the other hand, bishops who oppose personal dictatorships and institutional force, in their own country and elsewhere, point emphatically to the political relevance of the faith. In my view, these are the contrasts which, whether consciously or unconsciously, governed the conflicting views of the priesthood in the synod. The trend towards conservatism, the apolitical trend, was given strong support when to the surprise of many other representatives, Cardinal Höffner argued that it has not been established that the liberation of man from social and political alienation can be said to be an integral part of Christian salvation. But in plain language, this means either that the church cannot be bothered with the suffering endured by human beings as a result of institutions and structures (that cannot be the concern of a Christian), or that the church has a social, therapeutic function in respect of people who suffer in this way but that precisely because it is Christian it does not need to concern itself further with these structures. Without doubt it is difficult to make a precise definition, or to locate exactly the relationship between salvation or Christian redemption and human liberation. But salvation and redemption which does not take any tangible form in our historical dimension seems to me to be tantamount to supernaturalism and ideology.

Gaudium et Spes had already said that both a renewal of the mind and a reformation of social structures were demands on Christians (no. 26); and many fathers at the Council were so opposed to any division between the process of humanization and the growth of the kingdom of God that a key text in *Gaudium et Spes* was ultimately changed. In so far as this process is an instance of concern for our fellow human beings, an expression of *caritas*, one can never make an adequate distinction between dedication to a better and more righteous earthly future for mankind and dedication to the one thing that is necessary: God's honour shown forth in living man (see no. 39).[7] It is clear how the speech by Cardinal Höffner falls below the level already attained by Vatican II and betrays a conservative approach. I could point to more of these pre-conciliar signs in the synod.

They show that even Vatican II has not yet been assimilated. By this kind of speech and others in the same direction, some members of the synod dissociated themselves from those causes with which younger priests in particular identify themselves on the basis of their concern for mankind and their prophetic priestly function. It is hardly possible to imagine a clearer break between the tendencies noticeable in the synod and what can be found in the experience of many priests. An uncertain theology, lagging behind Vatican II, here got the better of a pastoral concern which, while seeing dangers, does not fearfully cut itself off from hopeful possibilities for the future.

This sacrificing of pastoral intentions to 'abstract principles' emerged most clearly in the discussion of the ordination of already married men as priests. From the speeches of those who represented the conferences of bishops it clearly emerged that, of the bishops spread out over the world, half, if not more, regarded the ordination of married men as a pastoral necessity (though their reasons for this might differ). However, when for the first time Cardinal Conway (Ireland) pointed to the danger of escalation – the ordination of married men would make a breach in the Latin law of celibacy and is in fact 'the beginning of the end' of the law – many bishops seemed to be seized with cramp. After this the principle of escalation was brought up dozens of times. Above all when Cardinal Seper suggested that this escalation was in fact envisaged and that for many bishops the 'ordination of married men' was simply a pretext for finding a way to *de facto* facultative celibacy after a generation, many people were not prepared to entertain even this minimal openness. In the name of a whole conference of bishops, some bishops made a passionate plea which in fact was taken as a pastoral *cri de coeur*. They said that they would be caught in a pastoral impasse if they had no possibility of ordaining married 'spontaneous leaders' of a community as priests. However, they fell silent under the threat of the principle of escalation. Furthermore, the fact that about nine members of the synod (in the name of their bishops' conferences) asked in so many words for the separation of ministry and celibacy and thus made a plea for facultative celibacy or for the possibility of two kinds of priests – married and unmarried – was the reason why the initial readiness also to ordain married men as priests by virtue of pastoral necessity, in countries where this seemed to be a pastoral imperative for the church, came to a standstill among some members with their *non possumus*: that cannot be. Cardinal Alfrink had seen through this social psychological mechanism beforehand, and therefore remained modest in his pastoral demands. However, even these modest demands in respect of his own church province sounded impossibly exorbitant. One bishop, who was apparently concerned only with Cardinal Alfrink's contribution, out of all the other speeches, said: 'One father, referring to collegiality, asked that this door should not be closed. For the sake of this same collegiality I ask that it should not be opened.' [8]

It is important to establish that no one in the synod attacked the intrinsic value of celibacy as a charisma. On the contrary. Although two members of the synod had questioned the law of celibacy simply on the grounds of human freedom (Patriarch Merouchi and the representative of the Bishops' Conference of Paraguay defended the most progressive standpoint in the synod),[9] even the so-called pastorally progressive bishops did not go so far. Instead of 'the law of celibacy' they preferred the expression: celibacy as a principle of selection for normal admission to the priesthood.[10] Although in actual practice this does not introduce any external change, a 'principle of selection' is nevertheless less liable to criticism than a law of celibacy associated with the official priesthood. However, given at least this general principle of selection (on the basis of an intrinsic affinity between ministry and celibacy) some people wanted the ordination of married men as well (not so much as a dispensation from this rule or purely because it was pastorally necessary or desirable, but) explicitly on grounds of substance, i.e. because of the particular value of the pastoral work of married priests and the fact that particular pastorates ask explicitly for married priests ('student pastorates' were given as an example of this by the Canadian bishops: speeches in the name of the Scandinavian episcopate by Mgr J. Gran, the Austrian episcopate by Mgr Johannes Weber, and the episcopate of Zaire [Congo-Kinshasa] by Cardinal Maloela, the episcopate of Ghana in a speech by Mgr P. K. Sarpong, and the episcopate of the Antilles in a shrewd speech by Mgr Sam Carter SJ, all pointed in the same direction). Disregarding their more prudent presentation, this was also the virtual drift of speeches like those of Cardinal Suenens, Cardinal Alfrink and Vicar General W. Goossens. By contrast, from the beginning the German episcopate adopted the standpoint that the (married) deacons were the appropriate leaders of the smaller grass-roots communities and that male and female pastoral lay helpers could provide for pastoral needs, at least in the present situation. Only when there had been thorough experimentation in this respect, a revision of the present priestly state and a transition to a differentiated pastoral ministry of men and women, could one consider the ordination of married men as presbyters – and that only if in the last resort all other expedients were of no avail. This is the thesis which was also accepted by the majority in the discussion groups.

One cannot deny a certain meaningfulness in all this. However, it is a meaningfulness within an *a priori* principle which was not discussed: cost what it might, no breach was to be made in the traditional discipline of celibacy in the West. Here the 'sign' was formalistically manipulated as a *sign* (even when in practice it no longer functioned as a sign). Mgr Sam Carter of Jamaica rightly said in the name of the bishops' conference of the Antilles that in the present situation married priests must stand alongside unmarried priests if in the eyes of the world the celibate priesthood is in fact to be a real sign. Despite all kinds of theoretical sophistry (especially the argument that the church does not compel anyone to become a priest), in the eyes of the world an obligatory coupling of celibacy with the priesthood is from a psychological perspective compulsory celibacy, as a result of which it loses its authentic force as a sign.[11] Bishop J. Gran of Oslo went even further and said: 'To close this subject allow me to say this:– if, – if we have the choice between having a sign and having priests, then let us have priests.' A sign which does not in fact function specifically and psychologically as a sign seems to these bishops to be an ideology: a suspect sign.

Thus this synod produces a precarious result. It is clear from the speeches of the bishops who formally represented their conferences of bishops that, given the particular needs and the particular cultural patterns of their local churches, the problem of celibacy cannot be solved uniformly and centrally in a single direction, whereas people wanted the synod to produce a unanimous judgment despite this. All the facts laid on the table point in the direction of a collegiate recognition of one another's needs and particular cultural patterns, and therefore in the direction of a prudential pastoral responsibility on the part of the bishops (in agreement with the Pope) within a homogeneous cultural sphere. There is a particularly apt illustration of this in two social and cultural patterns which take different directions: East Asia, and Ghana in Africa. In the name of the Ghanaian bishops, Mgr P. K. Sarong said that in accordance with the social ideas of his people a (spiritual) leader of a community needed to be married, because among them marriage was the sign of adulthood and possible leadership. This was so obvious that after a round trip another African bishop found that when he said goodbye to those whom he had visited they spontaneously sent greetings to his wife and children. He added, 'Only the catechists smiled. For the others, there was nothing unusual about it' (speech by Mgr J. Ndayen, Central Africa). On the other hand Cardinal Parecattil (Kerala), Mgr P. Nguyen-kim-Dien (South Vietnam) and others testified from the Eastern Asian cultural pattern with its already pre-Christian Buddhist evaluation of celibacy that a spiritual leader, a man of God, who was not *unmarried*, was tantamount to a squared circle. It was clear that a pluralistic solution to the problem of celibacy in the priesthood was a pastoral requirement.

However, the majority of the members of the synod were not convinced by this pastoral evidence. Why? If we analyse the tenor of the speeches that were made in the debates we can distil from them four basic reasons why the synod rejected the ordination of married priests, despite the wishes of a majority of the world's bishops. 1. The principle of escalation, in two senses: first, despite pastoral necessity ('we sympathize deeply with the heartache of some bishops', the Italian discussion group remarked in its report on the discussions that were held), the ordination of married men is nevertheless a breach in the Western discipline of celibacy and a first step towards facultative or freely-chosen celibacy; on the other hand, the concession of the consecration of married men in some provinces of the church would work as an 'oil slick' on other provinces – an 'infection', as some people put it; furthermore it would become a kind of social and psychological pressure on those priests who were still celibate. 2. The principle that at a time of crisis no fundamental changes should be introduced was invoked by many people after Cardinal Cooray of Ceylon had said, 'The hurricane is not the time to renovate the roof'. 3. The leadership of the church would make fools of themselves if five years after they had unanimously and solemnly renewed and reestablished a full obligation to celibacy, they were to go back on this principle at a synod (the same Cardinal Cooray). 4. The principle of the total availability of celibates, which was emphasized in most of the speeches (though the speakers were careful to keep quiet about the 'element of power' which is so much bound up with this concept). There is much truth in all this. And Cardinal Samore could support it with facts about the escalation of the married diaconate. The Dogmatic Constitution *Lumen Gentium* opened up the possibility of married deacons (no. 29) on condition that they had been examined and were 'of mature years'. Although in 1971 only twenty-five conferences of bishops had asked for permission to ordain married people as deacons, Cardinal Samore pointed out that requests were being made for the ordination of men who were thirty years of age and even younger. Furthermore, he added, there were already demands for dispensations for the remarriage of deacons whose wife had died. However, the real question is why there should be such panic fear of escalation. Without doubt it is humbug to praise the free charisma of celibacy verbally if in the last resort no one wants to pledge themselves to an apostolic celibacy. This makes talk about the value of the charisma of celibacy incredible. On the other hand, however, there would seem to be little confidence in what is called the ideal of the unmarried priestly life, if escalation can only be or will only be prevented by a legal prohibition. This absolute, rigid reliance on the law became all the more incredible in the eyes of many representatives because those who insisted on this law did not couple it with the reality of the availability required by the gospel, which involves poverty, the renunciation of power and titles of honour, and giving oneself away for fellow human beings, the features of religious celibacy which Superior General T. van Asten and some discussion groups in the synod after him, rightly noted. What is the sense of celibacy in a church in which members strive for honours, possessions and a comfortable middle-class life? Certainly, the official church may not approve of these things, but they are widely tolerated, and those whose life is marked by such privileges are not obliged to resign from the ministry as a result. 'What witness is given by a celibate priest, consecrated to God, if he has not renounced riches, ambition or honours? Would the care of children and the love of a woman be more dangerous for a priest than the care of riches or the smoke of incense? Why this strange lenience towards ambition, honour or riches . . . and this strictness over marriage?' (Superior General T. van Asten in his speech). In fact, failure to observe the law of celibacy is the only action which incurs an obligation to resign from the ministry, not the jockeying of priests and bishops for comfortable positions. Why? In other words, why this desperate attempt to hold back an escalation which to some extent – for anyone who retains their common sense – may in fact be a consequence of the ordination of married men as priests? Why not take account also of the positive aspect of some degree of escalation, as Mgr Sam Carter of Jamaica said? In the eyes of the world all priests are under suspicion of secretly 'wanting to marry, but not being able to', and in this way the sign that celibacy in accord with the gospel is a true possibility for living vanishes completely from the world.

An analysis of the speeches as they took place chronologically, one after the other, demonstrates quite clearly that the above-mentioned four themes in fact moved the synod in a conservative direction which did not match up to pastoral demands. Anxiety and rigidity – rather than pastoral concern, indeed even rather than concern for religious celibacy – made the majority of the synod, in contrast to at least half the bishops of the world, close their eyes to pastoral imperatives.

A certain ideology can be seen in all this. First of all, it must be remembered that some of those who in their speeches supported unqualified retention of celibacy for priests conceded that the motives for priestly celibacy presented so far did not carry any conviction, above all with younger men. Even those who believed in maintaining celibacy without qualification, *a priori* above discussion, thus advocating an 'unmotivated' principle of celibacy, beseeched the theologians to think of new and better motives for priestly celibacy. Another member of the synod said without further ado: if we do not impose the charisma of celibacy by law, it will not be put into practice;[12] here we can see the bankruptcy of the ideal which disguises other concerns. This ideological factor also played a part in another sense. When the doctrinal section was being discussed, as has already been said, many bishops were obsessed by the question how to draw an essential distinction between the activities of a priest and the pastoral work that the laity can and may do. Some even protested against the appearance of the laity in the pulpit. Nevertheless, when celibacy was discussed in the pastoral section, the same bishops often – in order to maintain unqualified observance of the law of celibacy, made a passionate plea that pastoral authority should be given to laymen, and suddenly even laywomen, in order to let as many ministerial services be carried out in the context of a shortage of unmarried priests. A cardinal, who (in the doctrinal section) had been concerned to limit preaching only to priests, suddenly said in the practical discussion: 'In the last resort it was the laity, and not the priests, who carried Islam over a great part of the world.' Furthermore, it seemed that the married laity (who would already have a job of their own) suddenly had to have total availability and would in fact have it, when of course this possibility had been ruled out in the case of married priests and limited only to unmarried priests. All this robs the synod of credibility. And even now I have still not said anything about the rather naive ideas about sex held by some members of the synod. One bishop took no trouble to disguise his ideology. A whole chorus of fathers at the synod began to argue in favour of relaxing the obligation to celibacy and ordaining married men, vying with one another in stressing the intrinsic and existential but not essential relationship between celibacy and priesthood. Whereupon this bishop pleaded with the others in God's name not to insist so fiercely on this relationship. For, he said, 'that may give some people the idea of looking for an affinity between marriage and the priesthood' (Mgr V. Mensah from Dahomey). Another bishop at the synod had meanwhile done that long before (Mgr M. Hermaniuk).

There was even mention of a degree of at least objective insincerity, both among some conservative bishops who kept quiet about the real situation in their dioceses, and among bishops open to pastoral needs. Cardinal Conway of Ireland cleverly pointed to this when he said, 'There are bishops who argue for a degree of separation of celibacy from the priesthood, but *non nobis, Domine, non nobis*; that is for other countries where it is necessary.' For some this was in fact an expression of collegial concern for the situation in other provinces; for others at the same time – given the situation as known from elsewhere – it was (in objective terms, at least) an act of insincerity, for fear of cutting a bad figure in front of the whites. That is understandable. Cardinal Seper, who by virtue of his office is well up with the situation in various parts of the world, said with sobering realism: 'I am not at all optimistic that celibacy is in fact being observed', and added, 'still less that marriage is', whereupon the conclusion followed quite logically: 'therefore celibacy must be maintained in full force'.[13]

It is obvious that in an age which is obsessed with sex people must also be aware of the commercial exploitation of sex and love and of the pressure this brings to bear on candidates for the priesthood. The synod did in fact have a sensible and critical word to say in this connection. But many members of the synod clearly looked on marriage in pre-Vatican II terms: as procreation and pure sex.[14] They said things about married ministers which were a slap in the face for many married, Reformed pastors. Some gave as a reason for not proceeding with too much haste to the ordination of married men: 'In the West we have no experience with married priests.' First of all, even within the context of the Western Catholic church this statement is incorrect: there is already some experience with married priests (above all Protestant ministers who have been consecrated priest with the Pope's permission). Furthermore, we have had centuries of experience of Protestant ministers.[15] If the concern was really to arrive at a well-thought-out, pastorally responsible decision on this practice, whether positive or negative, in connection with the question of the ordination of married men as priests (as the agenda of the synod envisaged), why were no observers invited from the Reformed churches (as they were to the Second Vatican Council)? Whatever the outcome of the synod, at least it would have been more credible. So we are compelled to say that there was no openness after the discussion because *a priori* – in whatever way – people did not want to change anything.[16] This makes a considerable amount of the open talk in the synod unbelievable, though we should not underestimate the consequences of this openness. Before the forum of the world it emerged that it was objectively desirable to have married priests. At least this openness towards the media is to the credit of this synod.

I have discussed the question of celibacy at some length, but this is completely in accord with the actual situation at the synod. Celibacy was in fact a test in which the synod had to choose whether it was uninfluenced by ideology, had pastoral concerns and wanted to illuminate the theological and theoretical implications of pastoral practice, or whether it had a contrary understanding, narrow 'orthodoxy' and a timid attitude which prevented brave pastoral involvement. An African bishop said, 'God's act of creation was also full of risks' (Mgr J Ndayer); he added somewhat grimly: if we do not have the courage to take risks now, 'Let us give up celebrating the

eucharist and baptizing, and tomorrow I will go and plant cab-
bages.' Later he was to say that he had not travelled thousands
of miles to join in the dancing in Rome.

Despite all this we should not minimize the valuable contri-
butions made by bishops in speeches at this synod. Thus for
example the Canadian episcopate, by virtue of its privileged
position in being represented by four bishops – in contrast to
e.g. Holland and Belgium, whose sole representatives could
each make only one speech on one theme – was able collectively
to present a coherent view of a *pastorale d'ensemble* by spreading
the speeches over four people. In pastoral terms this was far
superior to anything that the synod produced by way of documents or mere archives.

The synod debates on the question of celibacy nevertheless
marked quite clear progress from Vatican II in two ways: officially and psychologically. When there was a concern to reaffirm
the law of celibacy at the Second Vatican Council, in the first
instance about 400 bishops proposed the insertion, 'at least in
the present circumstances of the church'. This amendment was
rejected. Now this very same amendment was accepted by the
synod, at least in the discussion groups. The first proposition
which was accepted by the discussion groups with a two-thirds
majority ran as follows: 'On the ordination of married men.
Although this solution is theologically possible, it is neither
useful nor necessary at the present moment in the Latin church.'
The reason why it was not opportune at the present moment
was explained in these terms: 'first there must be a redistribu-
tion of the clergy; the possibilities of the permanent diaconate
must be explored; and finally, thought must be given to a
possible division of ministries and their differentiation through
lay participation.' Although a small minority wanted to vote
against the clause 'at the present moment in the Latin church',
in its discussion groups the synod thus in fact simply accepted
the continuation of the law of celibacy in full force for the
moment. Vatican II did not in fact go as far as this. Escalation,
however minimal, has begun officially here. Thus the pastoral
concerns expressed in the speeches in fact had some effect.

Furthermore, this was a social and psychological effect. First
of all, the bishops could speak out freely about the problems of
celibacy, and at greater length than the agenda really allowed.
Celibacy was not in fact on the agenda, but only the question
of the ordination of married men as priests. It was not the Pope,
but Cardinal Samore, who criticized the synod for going outside
its brief.[17] The Pope, who was present, tactitly allowed the

bishops to go beyond the limit that had been prescribed (because in the last result nine conferences of bishops asked in so many words for 'facultative celibacy'). In this way, in terms of social psychology the Rubicon was indeed crossed. Without doubt this is an escalation. The only question is how it is to be evaluated: in trust in the spirit of God, as a pastoral escalation, or in fear and pessimism at the evil world, as an escalation in the loss of norms and values. Although in our broken situation no motivation is completely pure and is always mixed, in real redemption Christian faith takes in both restricted motives and is therefore bold.

Meanwhile it can be regretted that by concentrating on the problem of the 'ordination of married men to the priesthood', members of the synod lost interest in all the procedural problems which still exist in connection with applications for dispensation from priestly celibacy. Only a few bishops called attention to the excessive and tedious bureaucracy here, and to the needless centralization for the settlement of this question. Almost mournfully and incomprehendingly Mgr F. Cheng-Ping Hsu, bishop of Hong Kong, gave a long account of this sorry procedure, ending, with Asiatic realism: 'If a man's priesthood no longer makes sense to him, or if he knows that he is unsuitable to continue as a priest and has resolved to resign, what point is there in his continuing for a single day longer?' The question of the use of defamatory language in this connection also came up on several occasions. Many priests have no intention of 'resigning their ministry'; they want to marry. If they do that, they are 'deprived' of exercising their ministry. That is the legal position, and to many people that is also psychologically the case. A few really want to resign, but many are actually given dispensations – these are two completely different things. None of this was adequately discussed at the synod.

In its final form, the synod's concept of the priest was expressed in nineteen propositions, of which only fourteen were accepted by the synod with the required majority (two-thirds of the votes). It is clear that both the final text on social and political involvement and that on the ordination of married men as priests did not satisfy either the majority or the minority, and therefore did not get the required majority. Furthermore, the first version of the final text on the ordination of married men as priests was so ambiguous that it was opposed both by the conservatives and by the pastorally more progressive. Against the practice of the Second Vatican Council, the list of amendments in the first instance was not communicated to the members of the synod; this only happened later, after a good deal of protest. I myself was no longer in Rome during the last week of the synod, but this week reminded me of the same situation at the end of the last session of the Second Vatican Council: some people wanted to prevent the formulation of a particular tendency, which at that time was strong. The same clear lack of clarity predominated during the last week of the synod. The responsibility for the ambiguous final text was shifted by one side on to the other. The *relator* responsible for the pastoral section of the concept of the priesthood himself had to say: 'I'm sitting uselessly in the middle.' The disagreement was so great that one bishop, Mgr Santos Ascarza (Chile), is said to have remarked that the one thing needed was a free discussion on facultative celibacy. In fact, tacitly this was the issue for the whole of the synod – whether the law of celibacy should be reaffirmed or 'opened up'. In the end, with Cardinal Munoz Vega as spokesman, the presidency conceded that the proposed final text was ambiguous. For clarification, therefore, the proposed proposition was to be divided into two separate final propositions, which were to be put to the vote: 1. 'It is proposed, subject to the consent of the Holy Father, that the ordination of married men to the priesthood shall not be allowed even in special cases.' 2. 'Only the Holy Father has the right, in special cases, out of pastoral necessity and for the general well-being of the whole church, to allow the priesthood to married men of mature years and a proven way of life.' The first proposition did not succeed in getting a two-thirds majority (only 107 for, out of 198 present who were entitled to vote); the second was even less successful (87 for, the others against, with two abstentions and two invalid votes). The ambiguity did not seem to be removed in these two propositions. The third proposition which was presented to the discussion groups is also typical: 'Given the shortage of priests in some communities and also for other pastoral and theological reasons, which make this new form of priestly ministry in some ways convenient, it seems opportune to recognize that conferences of bishops, with the approval of the Holy Father, should accede to the ordination of married men.'

Nevertheless, Mgr Lorscheider, a member of the amendments committee, explained the two-part proposition by saying that the expression 'in special cases' in the first proposition needed to be understood as applying to exceptional people (this is remarkable since the Pope had already been doing this for a long time 'in special cases'), whereas the expression 'in special cases' in the second proposition meant cases of local churches, so that the third proposition put to the discussion groups was obliquely implied in the final propositions one and two made by the synod, albeit in a more centralistic direction.

What seems to me to be even more illuminating is the fact that the insertion 'at the present moment in the Latin church', which was included in the first proposition approved in the discussion groups, despite the opposition of a small conservative minority, disappeared completely from the final version. This is clearly the work of the committee which produced the final drafts, against the trend of the synod itself. We might say that in the final version of the statements about the ordination of married men as priests, as a result of the final redaction, on this occasion we are confronted with an 'inbuilt' *nota praevia*: through simple omission. But despite its re-affirmation of the law of celibacy endorsed by Vatican II, in its final resolutions the synod simply expressed officially a malaise over the full enforcement of the Western obligation to celibacy. The result is meagre, but all the more significant for that reason: despite a general declaration of principle, only 54% of the members of the synod did not want any change in the unqualified continuation of this obligation to celibacy.

At the conclusion of the synod, Pope Paul VI said, 'We should give appropriate weight to the conclusions of the bishops when decisions have to be taken for the well-being of the universal church.'

The Synod of the Dutch Bishops in January 1980 simply confirmed the final conclusions of the Synod of Bishops of 1971.

(b) An evaluation of the 1971 synod

Where it was a matter of the priesthood, the 1971 synod was in fact obstructed by a burdensome heritage: not by the original doctrine of the Council of Trent on the priestly character, but by the way in which this doctrine in fact began to function after Trent in the church life of the West. As a result of a mistaken interpretation of Tridentine doctrine, the character became the feature which isolated the priest from the church community. The Second Vatican Council was extremely matter-of-fact in its reference to this character. It began from the priestly ministry which the Christian community itself requires (*Lumen Gentium*); it soberly adds: 'the sacerdotal office of priests is conformed by that special sacrament through which priests, by the anointing of the Holy Spirit, are marked with a special character' (*Pres-*

byterorum Ordinis, no. 2). Given the fact that in the time after the Council the functioning of the priest in the community came to occupy a central place in the specific experience of the priest, the post-Tridentine exaggeration of the character was as it were automatically 'displaced' by practice. The synod was a certain reaction against this.

This reaction seemed, however, to be ambiguous, because of the ambiguity of the conceptions surrounding this character, which moreover was regarded as a dogma of faith. Since Trent, the character had also been made the key concept of the priestly ministry. The character became as it were the 'ideology' of the priesthood.

At the synod, many bishops understood in the light of their pastoral practice that an ideology had grown up around the priestly character. But they also had sufficient Christian feeling to understand, without knowing precisely what this implied, that Trent must have meant something significant. Hence the uncertainty among the 'pastorally progressive'. Other bishops saw the only solution to the present-day problem over the priesthood to be a return to what they understood by the true teaching of Trent. This background obstructed the whole of the synod. Three bishops lamented at the synod: Do people have to ask us for a judgment on the precise significance of the character now, and on what the ministry must have been like in the early church?

Seen against the background of the universal tradition of the church in both the East and the West, what is the character of the priesthood but the 'charisma of the ministry' itself, which is called down on a believer who wants to commit himself to the official ministry of the church with the laying on of hands and *epiclesis* to the Holy Spirit in the name of the whole church community? Cardinal Suenens rightly stressed in the synod the pneumatological character of the ministry in the church, as many Eastern patriarchs who (in so far as they have not been Latinized) do not recognize the Western 'character'. And in that case it seems clear that the charisma of ministry is given as a function of a service to the community, a service which in fact requires complete personal dedication from the one who is called through 'the community of God'. Many priests who are dedicated to a believing community and are not burdened with a 'doctrine of the priestly character' thus show that in practice they have a deeper sense of what the traditional faith understands by 'character' than others who, making the most of a kind of *ordinatio absoluta*, defend the 'ontological character' verbally as the heart of the priesthood and do not know what it really comprises. This is where all the blockages arose in the debates in the synod. The priest is in fact 'bound to service' in the church community for his brothers and sisters, i.e. to the Christian community in its mission in the world, not simply through a personal will but through the Christian community and a charismatic gift of God, both of which transcend the priest as person. And once we realize that God and man, Christ and the Christian community – the 'body of the Lord' and the 'temple of the Holy Spirit' – while not identical, are nevertheless not diametrically opposed to each other, we shall not see professionalism and charisma as dilemmas, or, over and above all this, feel obliged to postulate an even deeper mysterious reality which is thought to make the priest a priest. That is to look for the mystery where it is not to be found, and to fail to see how the mystery of God is revealed precisely in the very lowly and profoundly human affairs of the church as a community and of the priest. In other words, in that case we fail to see the depth of the mystery and replace it with an ideology. Furthermore, this ideology is elevated to be the expression of orthodox Christianity. In this way polarization among believers is inevitably hardened.

In that case, must we not rather rejoice when young priests more than ever want to stand in solidarity with their fellow human beings in the church and in the world? Is this secularization? Or, despite the risks, is it not an insight into the true understanding of the priesthood, which arises through practice itself? The synod could have given so many priests encouragement, and could even have outlined a picture of the priesthood which younger men could again feel to be a real challenge. By missing this chance it inevitably provoked reactions which take up a good deal of time and energy that as a result are not available for the needs of pastoral work.

The procedure at the synod also made impossible a breakthrough in Christian pastoral work. Although it is not easy to devise another method of working, the procedure followed at the synod makes everything a matter of numbers. There is no discussion. Arguments are put on the table, but they are never discussed, nor is their strength tested. An argument which is advanced a great many times wins through in the end, no matter what its intrinsic value. An argument of high instrinsic value which is only presented once immediately gets discounted. The result of all this is that the editorial committee is given a position of virtual omnipotence. Although they are bound by the speeches in debate they can influence the final version quite fundamentally, above all depending on whether or not they take account of minority views. One feature of this synod in comparison with Vatican II was the almost striking difference in dealing with minority positions, depending on whether they were conservative or progressive.

The fact that arguments produced in a discussion are not analysed or tested as to their value is fatal in a gathering of two hundred persons. Thus dozens of times an argument was produced in terms of the 'general welfare of the church'. But what do we make of the fact that the pastoral needs of different local churches are sacrificed to this abstract term? Thus in the long run an accumulation of arguments which have not been analysed critically gives the impression of a massive witness, when perhaps not one of them actually holds water. Finally, leaving aside the arguments, a proposition is put forward which generally speaking reproduces something of what the quantitative majority has proposed: this quantitative result is then put to the vote.

While the result of the synod may thus have been negative, nevertheless the synod itself shows some division between the members of the synod and the conferences of bishops. At least half of the bishops spread over the world, if not more (as emerges from the speeches in the names of the great conferences of bishops) have a broader outlook and think in more progressive pastoral terms than the synod, at which their views were represented by a minority (albeit a strong one). That means that in at least half of its hierarchy the church wants to take a different course from that sanctioned by the synod. That is something in itself. On that basis it is difficult to attribute the new pastoral tendencies which were given modest expression in the synod simply to a few hot-headed priests or theologians, as often happens, without bringing at least half the episcopate of the Roman Catholic church into discredit. This makes one remark by Cardinal Seper very ambiguous, to say the least: 'Let me say clearly, that the pressure which is gradually becoming stronger and which comes only from a limited number of priests, in no way seems to me to be a sign of the times through which God is speaking to his church.' [18]

In addition to the division between the synod and the conferences of bishops there is a second division: that between some conferences of bishops and the priests who stand behind them. This was expressed above all in the remarks made by the conference of bishops in the United States, where the point was explicitly made. After giving a series of figures from which it seemed that a considerable majority of their priests thought in progressive pastoral terms, it was said that 'our conference of bishops does not share this view and had a different view of things'. This division seems to me to be more dangerous.

Nevertheless, anxiety and rigidity are forcing the church in the direction of a doubtful 'holy remnant' with a strongly-developed hierarchical top, whereas the real life of the Christian church flows elsewhere or is removed to the grass roots. In this sense the result of the synod was that the formation of grass-roots communities not only continued but became more intensive. In this way, against its will the synod gave new strength to the new trend which has been manifesting itself throughout the world for several years. The lack of interest in the synod and in problems which arise 'at the top' among many priests is striking in comparison with the first two synods. Many priests are finding their identity again in small Christian communities where they want to give a new form, authentic to the church, to the concept of priesthood, working it out in actual practice and sharing their responsibility with others. They are truly concerned with building up the church. Thus orthodoxy is given its best form in priestly orthopraxy.

2. The letter of Latin American priests to Pope John Paul II: July 1980

Before outlining some very general prospects for the future, I cannot do better than to quote the letter written by thousands of priests from Latin America to the Pope on the occasion of his journey to Brazil. It shows the challenge presented by the North-South problem to all Christian churches and gives an authentic echo of the gospel. It is also an expression of a trend in the church's ministry which will be significant as witness to the gospel in the service of mankind. Many Latin American bishops had already spoken in similar terms. Here, too, is a piece of living pastoral *magisterium*.

To Pope John Paul II, Bishop of Rome, who gives direction to the unity and neighbourly love of all churches:

Holy Father, we, priests of different churches in Latin America, address you on the occasion of your journey to this continent.

On this occasion you will be visiting Brazil. This is the country where the church makes an extremely important contribution to the future of the Catholic Church in Latin America and the rest of the world. It is a church which is born in the power of the Spirit and from the womb of the Lord's poor. From this church, which can be found throughout the continent, we want to express our faith and make a contribution to your visit.

Everyone knows the history of Latin America. But not everyone has had the same experiences. Some have been the conquerors and others the conquered. We want to begin to tell you our experiences and those of the people, because their voice is never able to be heard.

The first colonists found the original inhabitants of this land 'primitive' and 'uncared for'. That was sufficient justification for one of the most blatant cases of genocide in human history. The indigenous population was decimated and oppressed in the name of Jesus Christ. His cross, the symbol of redemption, took the form of the sword of the conqueror which was blessed by all but the good pastors of their church. This dishonouring of the gospel and the involvement of the church with the colonists and their system have been a source of serious ambiguities in the faith which still persist even now.

We believe that the time has come for the Catholic Church to confess its sins. It should acknowledge that it too was involved in Spanish and Portuguese colonization. We think that it must engage in self-criticism, which is without doubt healthy, especially for itself.

Three centuries after the independence of the Spanish and Portuguese colonies came the new 'colonists', the European interests. They let the world know that this was a divided continent. On the basis of this attitude it was split up into 'countries', despite the dream among some of its sons of 'one great fatherland'. This division served the interest of others, but certainly not that of the people, who were increasingly oppressed and were constantly kept divided.

After the First World War, as a result of the new international power structures, the political focal point was shifted to the northern continent. The United States of America announced the plans which it had for Latin America; for them we are and remain for ever an 'undeveloped' country within the capitalist system. As a result they again had a pretext for colonizing us. What was presented as brotherly help is in fact the plundering of our natural riches. And of course this cannot be without consequences. In contrast to what may be thought in other parts of the world, in Latin America the conflicts are not played out between church and state. Here we have the conflicting

interests of an exploited mass on the one hand and the state,
out for its own advantage, on the other. The conflict is thus on
the level of the oppressed people versus the ruling minority.

Part of this confrontation is also an arms race which is simply
a cover for instruments of oppression, which are constantly
refined; it also contributes to greater need among the exploited
majority.

In Brazil you will meet a people which is subject to the most
terrible material need and cultural poverty. You are aware of
the exceptionally high death rate among children, the illiteracy
and the premature deaths through endemic illnesses which
ravage our peoples. We simply want you to ask, as our people
ask, how this is possible in one of the richest countries in the
world.

Our people can easily find the key to an answer in the mech-
anisms manipulated by the great powers, and the imperialistic
politics which are supported by the Trilateral Commission.

They have no moral scruples, because their only 'morality' is
economic self-interest. So they never have sleepless nights,
either because of a genocide carried out in a highly subtle way
or because of the 'manipulation' by privileged groups on our
continent.

For this reason, too, there is no hesitation over helping military dictators into the saddle in the southern part of the continent, who indulge in bloody oppression. This is done under
the pretext of there being a 'power vacuum' and for 'the national
security', which only serves their own interests.

The people loathe the fact that their murderers appeal to their
own Christianity and use it as a justification for mass murders.
They loathe the fact that many bishops and even nuncios are
not without responsibility here, if only through their own
passivity.

At some time every people comes to the end of its patience,
and that end has now come for the people of Latin America.
Thus the people of Nicaragua have said 'Enough' to their dic-
tatorial government. The people of El Salvador and Guatemala
are looking for the means of securing their freedom.

This historical process in which our continent is now involved
is known throughout the world, but each person sees it in his
or her own way.

We, servants of Christ, incarnate in the story of the 'poor of
Yahweh', are certain that he is also alive on our continent and
eats bread with the hungry and thirsts for righteousness on
behalf of those of our people who live in prisons and suffer

torture and death in the fields. He is also present in the thousands of men, women and children who suffer from malnutrition.

Therefore we stand for true liberation and fight alongside the people in the name of this Jesus Christ.

Millions of brothers have gone before us in the same fight. Like them, we too are aware of the risks that we run and of the responsibility that we are taking upon ourselves. What Christ could not have suffered we are willing to suffer for him, for his body, the church, and as a proclamation of his resurrection. The proof of that lies with those who, in total surrender, have paid for this with their own lives.

Along with non-believing *companeros*, bishops too have fallen in the fight; and many sisters and priests, and thousands of Christians.

For us, the recent murder of Archbishop Romero in San Salvador is a symbol of this struggle and a witness which makes us tread in the footsteps of the good shepherd Jesus Christ, who gave his life for his sheep.

The death of Monsignor Romero follows the death of six priests in El Salvador in recent years. In Argentina in 1976, Bishop Enrique Angelelli de la Rioja paid for his 'choice for the poor' by his death, as did thirteen priests in that country. In Chile, three priests stand on the long list of those murdered by the military dictatorship which has been in power since 1973. In 1976 alone, two priests in Brazil paid for their witness with their lives. In Mexico, a country which is known on the continent for its respect for 'democratic freedoms', between 1976 and now three priests have been murdered. In Guatemala and Bolivia two priests have been killed in short succession, in each country, by the so-called established power.

To these 'extreme' testimonies of love we must also add those who for love have been exiled, imprisoned or tortured. At this moment dozens of priests in Latin America are in this kind of situation.

Illuminated by the example of this 'greatest love' of those who 'offered their life for their friends', and starting from the experiences of our oppressed and murdered brothers who keep demanding justice, we stress that our participation in this process is a biblical command and that we must therefore continue it.

On the other hand, those who represent opposed interests can see this model and this experience as a 'political' attitude in the bad sense of the word, or as being unworthy of the priestly ministry.

After Medellin, in Puebla the priests have again declared that they choose the side of the poor in this continent.

The poor of Latin America are not poor as the result of one kind of natural 'fortune' or another which has condemned them to perpetual need. On the contrary. As we have already seen, as producers, as farmers and workers, they are owners of an enormous potential of material wealth and cultural possibilities. Thus they are not asking any alms from the rich, but for a return of what has been stolen.

Thus one cannot call the cause of this situation 'humanitarian' or 'social'. It is a political cause, because there must be a radical transformation of structures which will put an end to the privileges of a small minority which maintains itself through great political and economic power.

Consequently we think that to 'choose for the poor' in Latin America is a political choice. That is the way in which it is understood by many Christians, and despite all the risks, we are prepared to keep our promise to the end.

With your visit to Brazil you will be coming for the second time to a continent at war. On the one hand is the exploited and oppressed class, which is constantly becoming more aware and is demanding rights which have been trampled on for so long. On the other hand are the privileged minority and the multi-nationals who harden their position and counter any attempt at the liberation of the people with fire and sword.

There must be an end to vagueness and neutral attitudes.

As servants of the same church of Jesus Christ, we hope that your visit means a renewal of the promise which the episcopate made in Medellin and Puebla; a clear and definite choice for the poor of Latin America.

We want to end with the words of our Bishop Martin Oscar Arnulfo Romero: 'The cry of this people for liberation is a cry which goes up to God and which nothing and no one can keep back.'

That is the letter.[19]

3. Prospects for the future

In this short historical and theological outline view of the ministry I have in fact already put forward the perspectives within which communities engaged in experiments can find the best structures of ministry, provided that there is periodical theological and sociological reflection on these experiments.

Along the lines of the ecclesial and spiritual dimension of a community I see the first requirement for the functioning of the ministry not primarily as a personnel plan or the recruiting of 'vocations', of ministers who, having secured the 'power of ordination', only need to wait for employment from the 'powers above'. I certainly see the need to develop a short-term pastoral plan for particular situations. In ecclesial terms: what must happen here, within this local pastoral unit, for the building up of a living community of men and women? In specific terms this means: what is the particular contribution of perhaps a small Christian grass roots community in the building up of a life of solidarity which is of a pluralist kind (and in which sooner or later people will feel the need to use the word 'God')? The more time goes on, the more this is the particular situation of a Christian community.

As in the early church, this coming community is a community of brothers and sisters in which the power structures which prevail in the world are gradually broken down. All have responsibility, though there are functional differences, and here at the same time there is a difference between general concern for the community and specific tasks of the ministry, above all that of the team leader(s) who coordinate(s) all charismatic services.

Only when an overall plan of the situation has been outlined can we see what kind of differentiated pastoral team is needed for smaller and larger pastoral units within a limited area. The model of the pastor who is capable of doing everything is clearly out of date. The agenda of a Christian community, the questions with which it should be concerned, are here for the most part dictated by the world itself. This gives a fourfold direction, dynamic and task to the inspiration of faith and in the light of this to the Christian action of a community (seen generally and schematically).

(a) A practical and hermeneutical or prophetic task

By this I mean that the community along with its ministers places the Christian tradition of practice and experience within the experiential and conceptual horizon (analysed and interpreted in a critical way) of those who live within a pastoral unit: i.e. preaching which relates the gospel to the present, catechesis within the context of particular experiences, interpretation of

the meaning of existence and history, an indication of the way
the community must go, and so on.

(b) The task of a Christian criticism of mankind and society

In the light of the liberating gospel, an attempt is made to trace
out those points where particular structures and prevailing attitudes obstruct rather than further freedom and humanity, and
thus hold back the coming of the kingdom of God. This includes
a political responsibility for the salvation of the community, and
of the community for the wholeness of the world.

(c) A diaconal task of Christian education

Here the building up of a community, as a catalyst in a pluralist
society, is experienced as a growth process which takes its
secular, human starting point in Christian participation in the
various forms of communal life which already exist outside the
church, in the neighbourhood of the pastoral unit. In this way
it is possible to avoid the formation of a ghetto or too much
looking inwards. Thus, there should be critical Christian solidarity with the work of social restructuring which is already
present, political involvement, and so on. Here the individual
pastorate should not be forced out. For all the specialization,
differentiation and restructuring of the ministry it would be an
ominous thing if there were no longer any pastors who helped
people in their desperate questions about meaning and their
perplexity in the face of the anonymous and official bureaucracy
of our modern life. Concern above all for the happiness of
particular people in their everyday lives is a task for the whole
of the church community, but especially for its minister. In that
respect the minister still remains a jack of all trades, and not
someone who can hide behind his 'pastoral specialization' or
his legitimate demand for a reform of the structures.

(d) A task of celebrating the liturgy and ultimately the eucharist

'How shall we sing the Lord's song in a strange land?' asked
the first despairing people when they lived in captivity in Ba-
bylon (Ps. 137.4). Must we not first liberate men and only later,
when they are freed, celebrate and sing of their liberation? With
the prophets in captivity in ancient times and also with today's
Latin American grass roots communities, communities and ministers can overcome their doubts in the light of very specific

experiences, namely that joy and prayer, singing and liturgy, while having their own intrinsic value and character of grace (so that they cannot be reduced to their effect on society), nevertheless also have a subversive effect in a world of disaster and oppression. Oppressors look to anxiousness and fear, bowing and scraping, to keep them in power, and not to happy songs of hope and love. In an evocative 'symbolic interaction' the liturgy expressly remembers and celebrates that in which the community has the basis of all its language and action. Secular and symbolic or liturgical forms of communicating meaning need one another and provoke one another. This means that the community, and thus its leaders, no longer locates the meaning of life and religious need so exclusively and so massively in the liturgy and the sacraments. In that case liturgical celebrations are more the obvious *kairoi*, privileged moments in the forming of groups and communities, and no longer an obligation; in fact they are spontaneous and nevertheless intrinsically necessary celebrations of the Lord's day, the day of men and women set free. In Latin America we Westerners were greatly moved when a crowd of nuns began in their usual way to express their happiness in song when they heard the Pope pronounce the word *allegria* (joy, happiness), so that in the end the Pope found it impossible to go on with his speech because every word contained an allusion to a song. Here a Christian community truly lived 'from below': the Pope's words were simply the words of a conductor: he indicated the melody (perhaps, though, to Western ears, there is a danger here of the medium becoming the message).

Together, these four tasks form a call to build up a 'Christian spirituality' of the community of God: 'Seek first the kingdom of God and his righteousness', i.e. act in accordance with the demands of this kingdom, especially those of a God who is concerned with humanity. For the sin from which Jesus has redeemed us extends over the whole of mankind, including his economic, social and political relationships, and not simply the inwardness of his heart. Thus to be called to the salvation which is given to us in Jesus also means realizing it in all these dimensions. False inwardness, i.e. an inwardness which is secluded from the outside world, is an illusion and gives no room for 'the powers of this world'. The only adaptation, the only *aggiornamento* that Christians know is a permanent adaptation of ourselves and the believing community to the life-style of the kingdom of God. But this adaptation, which is not an 'adaptation to this world', justifies a certain stress in the Christian spirituality of the community of believers in our time. The characteristic of our time and the context in which we live can be found in a paradoxical situation: within the church spirituality is still often proclaimed and practised in an unrealistic and non-materialistic sense (purely vertically, by means of prayer and contemplation), whereas on the other hand within the world social and political involvement is proclaimed as the only effective technology of salvation without reflection and wisdom, retreat and prayer. Thus our age imposes on the community of the church and its ministers the task of simultaneously stressing two points which serve to realize the authentic two-in-oneness of the Christian faith. This unmistakable duality is manifest in the one undivided personality of Jesus Christ. (*a*) On the one hand Jesus identifies himself with God's cause; the community is essentially concerned with God; (*b*) on the other hand Jesus identifies himself with man's cause; the community is essentially concerned with human beings and the life that they lead: spirituality is in the service of the humanity of men and women; (*c*) in the last resort these two things seem to be one and the same as far as Jesus is concerned; man's cause is God's cause, and God's cause is also man's cause. The contemporary Christian spirituality of a Christian community of faith can be recognized precisely in the way in which this is expressed through Jesus' central idea, 'the kingdom of God' among human beings.

This fourfold global dynamic of the spirituality of a Christian 'community of God' in its dimensions of religious prayer and religious political action, following Jesus within the specific horizon of local situations and within the wider horizon of the world, calls for appropriate and properly equipped leaders or leadership teams. In archaic terms we might call these presbyteral teams, as in the early church. Today we say the same thing by using the expression 'pastoral team', but that leaves the specifically ecclesial question of ministry obscure, if only to accommodate existing canon law. Leaders of the community in all kinds of differentiations and specializations fulfil a role in a variety of areas in directing, animating, guiding and inspiring. In fact they are 'significantly different' within the community, figures with whom to identify in terms of the gospel, in whom the community recognizes the best of itself and from whom it is also prepared to receive not only stimulus but also criticism, admonition and the comfort of the gospel, just as they too are prepared to receive stimulation, criticism and mercy from the community. This is precisely what the ancient church required of the ministry. This limited 'pastoral team', called or accepted by the community – after the testing of their whole way of life – must, in my view, also receive the *ordinatio* of the church, specifically in a liturgical celebration by the community which accepts it, with the laying-on of hands by the leadership teams from its own and neighbouring communities, with an epiclesis in prayer from the whole of the community. Given the specific and sometimes 'extraordinary' circumstances which can prevail, the laying on of hands, as acceptance by the church, bestowed on a member who is to be a leader in the community, seems to me to be the normal liturgical accreditation, in line with the first and second Christian millennia – for someone who is to preside over a community and thus over its eucharist. From a theological point of view this means that actual leaders of the community, who are also accepted by it, must also be given *ordinatio* or liturgical accreditation.

Here the sociological model of 'integrated leadership' seems to me to be valuable.[20] Of course even in the New Testatment the liturgical laying on of hands was polyvalent, and this was also true in the early church. It signifies the recognition through the community and its ministers, and those of neighbouring communities, of *de facto* leadership. This laying on of hands, as a result of which a charisma of ministry is recognized by the community or is asked of God, can do liturgical duty for all kinds of developments in practice. However much the tasks of the ministry may differ, the charisma of leadership prayed for or already present, and recognized in the laying on of hands, makes the question whether a particular minister may or may not do this or that (e.g. preside at the eucharist) an unnecessary puzzle. In the first three centuries, 'presbyters', who at that time were in no way ordained to preside at the eucharist, were allowed to do so with the permission of 'the priest' (i.e. the bishop). Given the circumstances, community leaders – of whatever speciality – can and may ultimately do anything that is necessary for the community as the *ecclesia Christi* on the basis of their ministerial *ordinatio* or institution. Furthermore, it seems to me to follow quite naturally from the New Testament that in extreme circumstances – for instance, given a total lack of ministers – an apostolic community can call one of their fellow Christians to be a minister to preside over them. However, on the basis of the whole history of the church's theology, I am opposed to a view which appears here and there, that any believer at all can preside at the eucharist even when leaders of the community ('priests') are present. This goes against the church's view of the ministry in the New Testament, the ancient church, the Middle Ages and the post-Tridentine period. Very exceptional circumstances in a community may not become the pattern for the normal life of an *ecclesia Christi* in the gospel, just as a particular view of the priest which has grown up in the course of history may not impede the vitality of the gospel.

Our age has rightly done away with the sub-diaconate and the so-called minor orders. However, we may well ask whether in the meantime we have not forgotten how to revive the ancient theological view which is implied by these orders: catechists in many countries, pastoral workers, who in many places in fact lead a community, are not recognized as such theologically or in church order. From an ecclesiological point of view this is an abnormal situation, which moreover leads to crazy consequences which even trivialize the eucharist. It is important here not only to take seriously the men and women pastoral workers, but also to recognize the ecclesial implications of their charisma (which is in fact that of a minister) accepted by the community: their *pneuma hegemonikon* or charisma of leadership. 'There is a multiplicity of gifts.' But all these gifts need to be coordinated on a larger or a smaller scale, 'to build up the body of the Lord' (Eph. 4.12).[21]

However, the fact is that the problem which has been raised is not understood at present in the same way in all the local churches of the Catholic community of faith. There is expectation of a complete theological and pastorally responsible 'solution'. Above all in central and northern Europe, people want a clear theological solution. In other countries, like French-speaking areas, Latin America and Africa, the dominant tendencies seem rather to be pragmatic; here people are not so much concerned over the academic question of *ordinatio* as with the fact that the laity are in fact those who give life to the faith of a community: the theological question of the official minister was then speedily solved with a reference to the concept of the 'extraordinary minister'. In the meanwhile it has become clear that 'Rome' has decisively refused the request that pastoral workers, whether male or female, should be given an *ordinatio* and not simply an *institutio* or *missio canonica*. Furthermore, the document of the synod of Dutch bishops in January 1980 (nos. 35 and 36) leaves no doubt that the central authorities of the Roman Catholic church directly reject an 'alternative' or, as the French put it, a 'parallel' church ministry. Rome does not want any new forms of the ministry alongside the episcopate, presbyterate and diaconate, and alongside the *ministeria* of acolyte and lector. Therefore the *de facto* leadership of the community by pastoral workers (who in some cases may be women) – regardless of whether these also preside at the eucharist and in other forms of sacramental ministry which are forbidden them according to present church order – remains theologically vague, and this is psychologically frustrating. Furthermore, as time goes on, the fact that to an increasing degree the whole inspiration for a Christian community lies in the hands of a theologically trained lay team, with a collaborating priest from elsewhere who comes to celebrate the eucharist, makes the actual presbyter a 'service type' for cultic affairs. This simply goes to strengthen the impression of the so-called Clichtove type of cultic priest who is a much more recent development in church history.

Some provinces of the church are very sympathetic towards an 'institutionalization' of so-called pastors; others are more cautious here. These 'pastoral workers' are often themselves frustrated, on the one hand because they are not positively inclined towards an *ordinatio* which in their view would clericalize them (which they certainly would not want), and on the other hand because their actual pastoral situation has not been completely 'institutionalized' (often it is also without appropriate legal, let alone financial guarantees).

From a purely dogmatic point of view, as has emerged from Chapter II above, the distinction between *ordinatio* and *institutio* or *missio canonica* is difficult to maintain. On the other hand, dogmatically it is just as clear that the only real ministers of the church are those who are recognized as such by the church; no one can take on himself the functions of the church's ministry on his own authority. The present theological disagreement and obscurity lies in the fact that on the one hand the supreme leadership of the 'universal church' has made it clear beyond all doubt that it refuses to recognize male or female pastoral workers as ministers of the church, while on the other hand in local communities the believing people with its presbyters who are already there in practice recognizes these *pastores* as *de facto* ministers (which used to be the essential feature of *ordinatio*). Thus from the point of view of the church's theology the situation is in fact very obscure, though in terms of church order it is extremely clear. The result of the official church concern for the 'identity of the presbyter' (in fact for the identity of the 'celibate' male priest) results in ambiguity and lack of clarity about the 'identity of pastoral workers (male or female)', who bear more of the burden of the community the more time goes on. This is not a healthy situation in any way, pastorally or theologically, above all because this official pastoral strategy of the church does not want to open the door by way of the pastoral workers to a non-celibate priesthood. A concern for what we can conveniently call the 'modern, Tridentine view of the priest' is scarcely an expression of concern for the actual living apostolic vitality of a creative Christian community. This is an attitude of pastoral strategy which raises serious historical and theological questions in the light of the eventful history of 'ministry in the church'.

A theologian cannot and may not take the place of the pastoral leaders of the church. By virtue of his task as a theologian, in critical service to the church, he has the sometimes painful duty of showing the church authorities whether their approach in fact takes into account all the features of what is actually a very complex set of problems. Here even the theologian in turn stands under the pastoral oversight of the leaders of the church; but this must not make him cowardly and prevent him from having his say. He must speak out even when he is convinced that in all probability the church authorities will make other decisions. Each person has his or her own unalienable responsibility for acting honourably and in accord with conscience, aware of the possible consequences which may follow, even for himself, in the church.

Abbreviations

BLE	*Bulletin de Littérature Ecclésiastique*
BZNW	Beihefte zur *Zeitschrift für die neutestamentliche Wissenschaft*
Conc	*Sacrorum Conciliorum nova et amplissima Collectio*
CSEL	Corpus Scriptorum Ecclesiasticorum Latinorum
HTR	*Harvard Theological Review*
JEH	*Journal of Ecclesiastical History*
JES	*Journal of Ecumenical Studies*
JQR	*Jewish Quarterly Review*
JTS	*Journal of Theological Studies*
LTK	*Lexikon für Theologie und Kirche*
NRT	*Nouvelle Revue Théologique*
NTS	*New Testament Studies*
OCP	*Orientalia Christiana Periodica*
PG	J. P. Migne, *Patrologia Graeca*
PL	J. P. Migne, *Patrologia Latina*
PWK	*Paulys Realencyclopädie*
RAC	*Religion in Antike und Christentum*
RSPT	*Revue des sciences philosophiques et théologiques*
RSR	*Recherches de Science Religieuse*
Schol	*Scholastik*
TvT	*Tijdschrift voor Theologie*
TQ	*Theologische Quartalscrift*
ZKG	*Zeitschrift für kirchengeschichte*
ZKT	*Zeitschrift für katholische Theologie*

Notes

Introduction 'No Church Community without One or More Leaders'

1. Jerome, *Dialogus contra Luciferianos*, ch.21: PL 23, 175.
2. See, *inter alia*, F. Klostermann (ed.), *Der Priestermangel und seine Konsequenzen*, Düsseldorf 1977.
3. See above all Jan Kerhofs, 'Priests and "Parishes" – A Statistical Survey', *Concilium* 133, 1980, 3–11; id., 'From Frustration to Liberation?', in *Minister? Pastor? Prophet?* SCM Press and Crossroad Publishing Co. 1980, 5–21; P. Zulehner, *Wie kommen wir aus der Krise? Kirchliche Statistik Oesterreichs 1945–1975 und ihre pastorale Konsequenzen*, Vienna 1978.

Chapter I The Story of New Testament Communities

1. I Thess 2.14; I Cor. 1.2; 10.32; 11.16; 11.22; 15.9; II Thess. 1.4; Acts 20.28.
2. Rom. 16.16; cf. I Thess. 1.1.
3. I Cor. 3.16; 6.19.
4. The figure 'seven' has a symbolic significance in Jewish thought. However, we might suppose that 'the seven' was a technical term for the 'council of elders', made up of seven, in the Jewish synagogue. Perhaps now Greek-speaking presbyters in Jerusalem are mentioned alongside the Christian council of presbyters made up of Aramaic-speaking Jews.
5. It is striking that 'Philip the evangelist' (Acts 21.8), one of the Hellenistic 'seven' (see also Acts 6.5), organized the mission to Samaria (Acts. 8.5, 12, 26–40) and other places on the Mediterranean coast among Greek-speaking Diaspora Jews, with Caesarea as a centre.
6. Acts 1.21f; cf. Luke 24.36–39.
7. In the so-called 'Niceno-Constantinopolitan creed'; however, this is in fact an Eastern baptismal creed which later came into general currency. The qualification 'apostolic' was inserted into the description of the 'one, holy and catholic church' at a time when Christians were in danger of forgetting the historical origin of the Christian communities and were involving themselves too much in speculation. Emphasis was laid on this apostolicity even in the later New Testament period

as a counter to excessive speculation (albeit in an incipient 'doctrinal' sense); Jude 3; II Tim. 1.13, 14; 3.14; Titus 2.1; I Tim. 3.13; 4.1, 6; 6.3, 12, 20; II Tim. 2.2, 15, 18; 3.8ff.; Titus 1.13f.

8. In other New Testament texts also the leaders of the community still do not seem to have any official name, or are referred to by names which vary from community to community, which is why they are generally called 'those who lead you', 'those who labour for you', etc. (I Thess. 5.12; Rom. 16.6, 12; also Heb. 13.7, 24).

9. As is well known, the tripartite division into apostles, prophets and teachers (or wise men) is of Jewish inspiration. The apostles as it were lay the foundation of the 'law of the gospel' (see Matt. 5.1ff.; II Cor. 3.4–11; Luke 6.12ff.; Acts 15.21). Paul, who does not make a very convincing systematic theologian in this respect, tries to synthesize this into the triad: (*a*) varieties of charismata, deriving from one pneuma; (*b* varieties of *diakoniai* or services, in the service of one Lord; (*c*) varieties of *energemata* or activities, as the fruit of one and the same God (I Cor. 12.4–6): 'each . . . for the common good' (I Cor. 12.7). 'Prophets' played a considerable part in the first Christian communities (the details of which cannot now wholly be recovered). The writer of the book of Revelation still calls himself a 'prophet' (Rev. 1.3; 10.7; 22.18f.) and ultimately writes 'prophetic letters' (Rev. 2.1 – 3.22) and 'extraordinarily prophetic', i.e. specifically 'apocalyptic' letters (Rev. 4.1–22). See also the role of the prophets in Luke's account of Paul's journey from Corinth to Jerusalem (Acts 20.3 – 21.17). The spirit of the prophets is the 'spirit of Jesus' (Acts 16.7; Phil. 1.19), who was felt to be a prophet before he was recognized as Messiah.

10. 'Pastors' (Eph. 4.11) probably has no specific significance for a differentiated ministry. It is an image of feeding the flock (John 21.15–17; Acts 20.28; 20.35a; I Peter 5.14). Jesus is called the arch-pastor (I Peter 5.4; see 2.25). Only in the post-apostolic period as represented by the New Testament does pastor – also directed against the heretics (Acts 20.28) – become a general term for all church officials (Eph. 4.11; Acts 20.28; I Peter 5.1–4; see also Matt. 16.18f.; 18.18; John 20.22f.).

11. See, *inter alia*, N. Brox, *Pseudepigraphie in der heidnischen und jüdisch-christlichen Antike*, Darmstadt 1977, and W. Speijer, 'Die literarische Fälschung im Altertum', in *Handbuch der Altertumswissenschaft* I–1, Munich 1971.

12. See F. Prast, *Presbyter und Evangelium in nachapostolischer Zeit*, Forschung zur Bibel 29, Stuttgart 1979; E. Nellessen, 'Die Einsetzung von Presbyters durch Barnabas und Paulus (Apg. 14, 23)', in *Begegnung mit dem Wort*, ed. J. Zmijewski and E. Nellessen, Festschrift H. Zimmermann, Bonn 1980, 175–94; J. Michl, 'Die Presbyter des ersten Petrusbrief', in *Ortkirche-Weltkirche*, Festschrift J. Kard. Döpfner, Würzburg 1973, 48–62.

13. R. Brown, *Priest and Bishop*, New York 1970, 33ff.; 63ff.

14. *Ordinatio* or institution, later called consecration, is a Christian reinterpretation of the Jewish *ordinatio* of a rabbi. After he had been instructed by a rabbi, hands were laid on a rabbinic candidate by his

teacher – in the presence of two rabbis as witnesses (following the model of the installation of Joshua by Moses, Num. 27.21ff.; although we only find assured literary evidence for this consecration of a rabbi about AD 75, it is at all events before the Christian Pastoral Epistles). The purpose of the Jewish consecration of a rabbi was that the wisdom of the teacher should pass over to the rabbinic candidate, who from that point on might also call himself a rabbi (teacher); it guaranteed continuity with the Mosaic law-giving, though he could interpret this tradition independently (see E. Lohse, *Die Ordination im Spätjudentum und im Neuen Testament*, Göttingen 1951; K. Hruby, 'La notion d'ordination dans la tradition juive', *La Maison-Dieu* 102, Paris 1970, 52–72; A. Ehrhardt, 'Jewish and Christian Ordination', *JEH* 5, 1954, 125–38; G. Kretschmar, 'Die Ordination im frühen Christentum', *Freibürger Zeitschrift für Theologie und Philosophie* 22, 1975, 35–69.

15. From Acts 20.17, compared with 20.28, and I Peter 5.5, compared with 5.2, it seems that *episkopoi* and *presbyteroi* are the same people. Titus 1.6ff. also suddenly mentions an *episkopos* in a context which is concerned with *presbyteroi*. Furthermore, in I Clement 44.1, as compared with 44.5, the *episkopos* is obviously a *presbyteros*. However, the so-called 'monarchical episcopate' is not a biblical norm, although it is a legitimate form of church order.

16. Ignatius, Magn. 2; 3.1; 4; 6.1; 7.1; Trall. 2.2–3; 3.1; 7.2; Smyrn. 8; Polyc. 5.2; ad Phil. 4. For years historians have tended to give a late date to the model of the so-called monarchical episcopate which it is difficult to place early. This is connected with the grave historical suspicions attached to an early dating of writings which had been ascribed to Ignatius of Antioch. The longer they go on, the more convincing are the arguments that this monarchical episcopate should be dated much later. See A. Davids, ' "Frühkatholizismus" op de helling: rond de brieven van Ignatius', *TvT* 20, 1980, no. 2, 188–91.

17. Since there are those who elevate the 'episcopate' and the 'presbyterate' to an apostolic norm because they occur in the New Testament (at the same time forgetting that both the distinction between them and their content is far from clear in the New Testament), why is there not also a remembrance that in the same way the Pastoral Epistles presuppose that the *episkopoi-presbyteroi* and deacons are always married? And in I Cor. 9.4–6, Paul even talks about the right of the apostles to be married. There is no hermeneutical justification for such selectivity in the use of the Bible. The question is what the New Testament itself means to affirm as a norm, and in the Pastoral Epistles this is merely the principle of apostolicity and not the specific structuring of the ministries.

18. I might recall here that even in the Middle Ages, despite the dispute between *regnum* and *sacerdotium* (emperor and pope), all great theologians from the thirteenth century explicitly reject the position of power of the church's ministry (see Ch. III, n. 9).

19. E. Schweizer, *Church Order in the New Testament*, SCM Press 1961, 117–38.

20. K. Donfried, 'Ecclesiastical Authority in 2 and 3 John', in *L'Evangile de Jean* (ed. M. de Jonge), Gembloux 1977, 325–33.

21. W. C. van Unnik, 'The Authority of the Presbyters in Irenaeus' Works', in *God's Christ and His People*, Festschrift N. A. Dahl, ed. J. Jervell and W. A. Meeks, Oslo 1977, 248–60; J. Munck, 'Presbyters and Disciples of the Lord in Papias', *HTR* 52, 1959, 223–43.

22. H. Schlier, 'Der Hl. Geist als Interpret nach dem Joh-evange-lium', *Communio* 2, 1973, 97–108; R. A. Culpeper, *The Johannine School*, Missoula 1975, 265–70; R. Brown, *The Community of the Beloved Disciple*, New York 1979; M. de Jonge, *Jesus: Stranger from Heaven and Son of God*, Missoula 1977; D. M. Smith, 'Johannine Christianity', *NTS* 21, 1974–75, 228–48; H. Conzelmann, 'Was von Anfang war', *Neutestamentliche Studien für R. Bultmann*, BZNW 21, Berlin 1954, 194–201; J. O'Grady, 'Individualism and Johannine Christology', *Biblical Theology Bulletin* 5, 1975, 227–61, and 'Johannine Ecclesiology. A Critical Evaluation', *Biblical Theology Bulletin* 7, 1977, 36–44.

23. De Jonge, op. cit., 205.

24. R. Brown, op. cit., 160.

25. See E. Ruckstuhl, 'Zur Aussage und Botschaft von Johannes 21', *Die Kirche des Anfangs*, Festschrift H. Schürmann, ed. R. Schnacken-burg, Leipzig 1977, 339–62, esp. 360f.

26. See already Ignatius, Smyrn. 8.1; 9.1; Eph. 5.3; Trall. 2.1. See Ch. I, n. 16.

27. In this connection see a recent book, *Das Recht der Gemeinde auf Eucharistie. Die bedrohte Einheit von Wort und Sakrament*, edited by the Solidaritätsgruppe katholischer Priester der Diözese Speyer, Trier 1978.

28. In *Das Recht* (see n. 27 above), J. Blank defends the position that from the perspective of the New Testament the eucharist is really 'outside the ministry'. I think he is wrong. The position is indeed that in the New Testament the ministry did not develop from and around the eucharist, but from and around the formation of the community. However, I would add that it did so from the way in which the apostolic communities took shape by a practical 'discipleship of Jesus', after the fashion of the apostles.

29. See K. Hruby, 'La "Birkat ha-mason" ', in *Mélanges Liturgiques*, Louvain 1972, 205–22; L. Finkelstein, 'The Birkhat Ha-mazon', *JQR* 19, 1928–29, 211–62; T. Talley, 'De la "Berakah" à l'eucharistie', *La Maison-Dieu* 125, 1974, 199–219.

30. See J. Audet, *Le Didaché*, Paris 1958.

31. See the literature cited in Ch. II, n. 27.

32. E. Schillebeeckx, *Christ*, SCM Press and Crossroad Publishing Co. 1980, 262–6.

33. In I Cor. 12.28, ministries are mentioned in the midst of all kinds of other forms of service.

Chapter II   Ministry in the First and Second
Christian Millennia

1. PG 104, 558; commentary PG 104, 975–1218; 137, 406–10. See the editions by: P. P. Joannou, *Discipline générale antique*, I–1, *Les canons des conciles oecuméniques*, Grottaferrata 1962, 74f. Latin translations: E. Schwartz, *Acts Conciliorum Oecumenicorum: Concilium generale Chalcedonense* II, 2, 2, Berlin and Leipzig 1936. Explanatory literature: V. Fuchs, *Die Ordinationstitel von seiner Enstehung bis auf Innocenz III*, Bonn 1930; Cyrille Vogel, *'Vacua manus impositio:* L'inconsistance de la chirotonie en Occident', in *Mélanges Liturgiques*, offerts au R. P. Dom B. Botte, Louvain 1972, 511–24; J. Martin, *Die Genese des Amtspriestertums in der frühen Kirche, Quaestiones disputatae* 48, Freiburg 1972; A. Lemaire, *Les Ministères dans l'Eglise*, Paris 1974, and *Les Ministres aux origines de l'Eglise*,Paris 1971.

2. Gregory VII, *Reg.* IX, 3 and 18. See G. Fransen, in *Etudes sur le sacrament de l'Ordre*, Paris 1957, 259f.; P. M. Gy, ibid., 125f.; P. van Beneden, *Aux origines d'une terminologie sacramentelle ordo, ordinare, ordinatio dans la littérature latine avant 313*, Louvain 1974; M. Bevenot, 'Tertullian's Thoughts about the Christian Priesthood', in *Corona Gratiarum*, Miscellanea E. Dekkers, Vol. 1, Bruges 1975, 125–37; P. Fransen, s.v. 'Ordo', *LTK²* VII, 1212–20: B. Kübler, 'Ordo', in *PWK* XVIII, 1, Stuttgart 1939, 330–934.

3. T. Klauser, *Der Ursprung der bischöflichen Insignien und Ehrenrecht*, Krefeld ²1953. This leads later to an *ordo clericalis* and an *ordo laicalis*, *Decretum Gratiani* IV, q.1, c.2: Friedberg 537). In Victorine theology *ordo* becomes the *sacramentum ordinis* (Hugo of St Victor, *De Sacramentis* II, 2, 5: PL 176, 419).

4. Leo the Great, *Ad Anast.*: PL 54, 634. See L. Nortari, *Consecraziòne episcopale e collegialità*, Florence 1969; H. Dombois, *Das Recht der Gnade*, Witten 1961; R. Kottje, 'The Selection of Church Officials', *Concilium* 7, 1971, no. 3, 117–126; H. M. Legrand, 'Theology and the Election of Bishops in the Early Church', *Concilium* 8, 1972, no. 7, 31–42.

5. Cyprian, *Epist.* 67.4; 61.3; 73.7.

6. Cyprian, *Epist.* 4.5; PL 50, 434. See F. Nikolasch, *Bischofswahl durch aller konkrete Vorschläge*, Graz-Cologne 1973; K. Ganzer, *Papsttum und Bistumbesetzungen in der Zeit von Gregor IX bis Bonifaz VIII*, Cologne 1968, which shows the historical circumstances which led to a break with the old church order.

7. Leo the Great, *Ad Anast.*: PL 54, 634. This also says that 'No one may consecrate a man bishop against the wish of the Christians and unless they have explicitly asked for this.'

8. Paulinus, *Epist. I ad Severum*, ch. 10: CSEL 29, 9.

9. Isidore, *De ecclesiasticis officiis* II, 3: PL 83, 779.

10. *Vita Hieronymi*, XII, 3: PL 22, 41.

11. Leo, *Epist.* 167: PL 54, 1203; Burchard of Worms, *Decretum*: PL 140, 626; Ivo of Chartres, *Decretum* VI, 26: PL 161, 451: *Decretum Gratiani* I, d. 70, ch.1; ed. Friedberg I, 254; Council of Pavia (850), in Mansi,

Conc. XIV, 936; Council of Piacenza (1095), in Mansi, *Conc.* XX, 806; Hugo of St Victor, *De sacramentis* II, p. 3, ch. 2: PL 176, 421.

12. There was some discussion over the legitimacy of the 'chorepiscopi'. To begin with, bishops lived only in cities: at that time 'chorepiscopi', or country bishops, had a territory or a local community that was difficult to define; hence the uncertainty. At all events this points overwhelmingly to the ecclesial conception of the office. See A. Bergère, *Etudes historiques sur les chorévêques*, Paris 1925; T. Gottlob, *Der Abendländische Chorepiskopat*, Amsterdam 1963; G. Fahrnberger, *Bischofsamt und Priestertum in den Diskussionen des Konzils van Trient*, Vienna 1970.

13. A cogent historical demonstration of this seems to me to have been given by Cyrille Vogel, '*Laica communione contentus*: Le retour du presbytre au rangs des laïcs', *RSR* 47, 1973, 56–122.

14. *La Tradition apostolique de saint Hippolyte* (Liturgiewissenschaftliche Quellen und Forschungen 39), ed. B. Botte, Munster 1963 (= *Sources chrétiennes* 11 bis), 113–26; B. Botte, 'L'ordination de l'évêque', *La Maison-Dieu* 98, Paris 1969, 113–26; id., 'La formule d'ordination "la grace divine" dans les rites orientaux', *L'Orient Syrien* 2, 1957, 285–96; id., 'L'ordre d'après les prières d'ordination', in *Etudes sur le sacrament de l'ordre*, Paris 1957, 13–35; A. Rose, 'La prière de consécration par l'ordination épiscopale', *La Maison-Dieu* 98, Paris 1969, 127–42; C. Vogel, 'L'imposition des mains dans les rites d'ordination en Orient et en Occident', *La Maison-Dieu* 102, Paris 1970, 57–72; id., *Le ministère charismatique de l'eucharistie*, Studia Anselmiana 61, Rome 1973, 181–209; J. Lecuyer, 'Episcopat et presbytérat dans les écrits d'Hippolyte de Rome', *RSR* 41, 1953, 30–50; H. J. Schulz, 'Das liturgisch sakramental übertragene Hirtenamt in seiner eucharistischen Selbstverwirklichung nach dem Zeugnis der liturgische Ueberlieferung', P. Bläser et al., *Amt und Eucharistie*, Paderborn 1973, 208–55; id., 'Die Grundstruktur des kirchlichen Amtes im Spiegel der Eucharistiefeier und der Ordinationsliturgie des römischen und des byzantischen Ritus', *Catholica* 29, 1975, 325–40; H. M. Legrand, 'Theology and the Election of Bishops in the Early Church', *Concilium* 8, 1972, no. 7, 31–42; J. H. Hanssens, 'Les oraisons sacramentelles des ordinations orientales', *OCP* 18, 1952, 297–318; U. Brockhaus, *Charisma und Amt*, Wuppertal 1962, 674–6; V. Fuchs, *Der Ordinationstitel von seiner Enstehung bis auf Innocenz III*, Bonn 1930; G. Pinto de Oliviera, 'Signification sacerdotale du ministère de l'évêque dans la Tradition Apostolique d'Hippolyte de Rome', *Freiburger Zeitschrift für Theologie und Philosophie* 25, 1978, 398–427.

15. Hippolytus is a Christian author writing from Rome, leader (presbyter?, bishop?, even anti-pope?) of a Christian community which had a controversy with Pope Pontianus (231–235). At this time the liturgies had not yet been fixed; people improvised on canvases which were in one sense established. Hippolytus gives specific models which more than probably reflect the Roman liturgy of the beginning of the third century. This model is the earliest Christian liturgy known to us;

it also circulated in the patriarchates of Alexandria and Antioch. At that time Greek was still the official language in Rome; only individual fragments of the Greek have been preserved, but in addition we have the complete, very slavish Latin text (which suggests the individual Greek even down to details), and also a number of other ancient translations.

16. *Traditio* 2: Botte (1963 ed.), 4–11. From Ps. Dionysius onwards the prayer to the Holy Spirit at the *ordinatio* was called *epiklesis* (*De Eccl. Hierarchia* 5, 2: PG 3, 509).

17. Y. Congar, 'Ordinations "invitus", "coactus", de l'Eglise antique au canon 214', *RSPT* 50, 1966, 169–97. The consequences of this pressure are analysed in a detailed study, above all when from the end of the fourth century the senior clergy in the West were obliged to be completely celibate: P. H. Lafontaine, *Les conditions positives de l'accession aux ordres dans la première législation ecclésiastique (300–492)*, Publications sériées de l'Université d'Ottawa 71, Ottawa 1963, esp. 71–100. Moreover it emerges from this study that even at this time the community still always chose its presbyters itself (until often fights broke out when the wishes of the believers were not honoured).

18. *Constitutiones Apostolorum* 8 (F. X. Funk, *Didascalia et Constitutiones Apostolorum* 1, Paderborn 1905).

19. 'Apostolicity' in the sense of ch. 1.

20. Nevertheless, it should be remembered that even in the third century there was considerable caution about sacerdotalizing, in whatever form, of the ministry: only Christ and the people of God are priestly. Hippolytus himself therefore repeatedly says: the bishop (= *sacerdos*) is like a high priest (*Traditio* 3 and 34). The presbyters are still not priests (*sacerdotes*), although they may preside at the eucharist with the bishop's permission (at least in many church provinces). This practice increases as time goes on. In the ancient church, to begin with *sacerdos* was applied to the bishop purely in Old Testament and allegorical terms. After that it gradually came to be used in a real sense. Generally speaking, down to the fifth century *sacerdos* usually means the bishop. (See P. M. Gy, 'La théologie des prières anciennes pour l'ordination des évêques et des prêtres', *RSPT* 58, 1974, 599–617; Schillebeeckx, s.v. 'Priesterschap', in *Theologisch Woordenboek* 3, esp. 3974f.). In the West, *sacerdotes secundi ordinis* is common from the fourth and fifth centuries onwards (see B. Botte, '*Secundi meriti munus*', in *Questions Liturgiques et Paroissales* 21, 1936, 84–8); at the end of the fourth century and the beginning of the fifth bishops were also called *archiereis* and presbyters *hiereis* in the East. The *Apostolic Tradition* of Hippolytus is still in a tradition which calls only the bishop 'priest'. In other words, before the time of Nicaea the term 'presbyter' may not in any instance be translated as 'priest'.

21. For the Jewish background to *ordinatio* see the literature in Ch. I, n. 14.

22. *Traditio* 7: Botte, ed. 1963, 20f. (See B. Botte, '*Presbyterium et ordo episcoporum*', *Irenikon* 29, 1956, 3–27).

23. Gy, 'La théologie des prières anciennes'.

24. *Traditio* 8: Botte, op. cit., 22–7.

25. *Traditio* 9; ibid., 28f.

26. *Traditio*, 11 and 13; ibid., 30 and 32. In the *Constitutiones Apostolorum* 8, 21, 2 and 8, 22, 2 (Funk I, 525), the sub-deacons and lectors also receive the laying on of hands (about the end of the fourth century). See also K. Rahner and H. Vorgrimler (eds.), *Diaconia in Christo*, Quaestiones disputatae 15/16, Freiburg im Breisgau 1962, 57–75.

27. 'Non imponetur manus super eum ad diaconatum vel presbyteratum. Habet enim honorem presbyteratus per suam confessionem. Sin autem instituitur episcopus, imponetur ei manus' (*Traditio*: Botte, ed. 1963, 29f.). Botte denies that the suffering *confessio* (*martyrium*) takes the place of an ordination (however, a distinction should be made here: it is certainly liturgical institution but without the laying on of hands); C. Vogel, 'L'imposition des mains dans les rites d'ordination en Orient et en Occident', *La Maison-Dieu* 102, 1970, 57–72, takes the same line as Botte. We do not find adequate explicit references outside the *Traditio*, but in antiquity what seems to Western men who grew up with later scholastic presuppositions to be liturgically impossible may itself have been taken for granted! In the ministry, the early church was primarily concerned with the gift of the charisma of the spirit, which to begin with was itself purely charismatic, though here too (as also in the New Testament), the *receptio ecclesiae* was always a factor. Tertullian says, 'Christus in martyre est' (*De pudicitia* 22, 6; cf. Cyprian, *Epist.* 40). See M. Lods, *Confesseurs et Martyrs, successeurs des prophètes dans l'Eglise des trois premieres siècles*, Paris-Neuchâtel 1950; D. van Damme, 'Martus. Christianos. Überlegungen zur ursprünglichen Märtyrentitel', *Freiburger Zeitschrift für Philosophie und Theologie* 23, 1976, 286–303. The laying on of hands is certainly necessary for the episcopacy of confessors (*Traditio* 9; Botte, op. cit., 28f.).

28. It is of interest in this respect that the *doctores* or teachers in Hippolytus' *Traditio*, 15 and 19 (Botte, ed. 1963, 32 and 40) – he is referring to the leaders of the catechumenate – could be either clergy or laity (above all *Traditio* 19), and that at the end of the religious instruction both the lay teacher and any ordained teacher there could lay hands on the catechumens. Thus the *didaskaloi* are not ordained *per se*.

29. Cyrille Vogel, 'Chirotonie et Chirothésie', *Irenikon* 45, 1972, 207–35, and, 'Unité de l'Eglise et pluralité des formes historiques d'organisation ecclésiastique du IIIe au Ve siècle', in *Episcopat et l'église universelle*, Unam Sanctam 39, Paris 1964, 591–636.

30. Jerome, *Epist. 146 ad presbyterum Evangelium*, CSEL 56, 310. Here we must remember that at least Jerome did not estimate the laying on of hands all that highly (*Comm. in Isaiam* 16.58, 10: PL 24, 569).

31. C. Vogel, 'Chirotonie', 20f.

32. An authoritative historian like C. Vogel can happily write: 'C'est la preuve, à n'en pas douter, que l'essentiel n'est pas le rite d'ordination, la chirotonie, mais le fait que l'Eglise reconnait, même sans

imposition des mains, comme presbytres ceux qu'elle veut bien accuellir: c'est la "reconnaissance" comme ministre de l'Eglise, le mandat que fait le clerc, non la chirotonie' (Vogel, op. cit., 21).

33. Leo I, *Ep. ad Rusticum*: PL 54, 1203.

34. See V. Saxer, *Vie liturgique et quotidienne à Carthage vers le milieu du IIIe siècle*, Rome 1969, 194–202; A. Janssen, *Kultur und Sprache. Zur Geschichte der alten Kirche im Spiegel der Sprachentwicklung von Tertullian bis Cyprian*, Nijmegen 1938.

35. '*Sacerdos vice Christi vere fungitur*' (Cyprian, *Litt.* 63: PL 4,386). See B. D. Marliangeas, *Clés pour une théologie du ministère*, Paris 1979, 47.

36. Augustine, *Contra Ep. Parmeniani* II, 8, 15 and 16: *CSEL* 51, 1908 (PL 43, 49–50).

37. See P. M. Gy, 'La théologie des prières anciennes pour l'ordination des évêques et des prêtres', *RSPT* 58, 1974, 599–617.

38. B. Botte, '*Secundi meriti munus*', in *Questions Liturgiques et Paroissales* 21, 1936, 84–8.

39. Tertullian, *De Corona* 3. See also Justin, *Apology* I, 65, 3 and 67, 5; A. Quacquarelli, 'L'epiteto sacerdote (hiereis) ai crestiani in Giustino martire, *Dial.* 116, 3', in *Vetera Christianorum* 7, 1971, 5–19. See C. Vogel, 'Le ministère charismatique de l'eucharistie', in *Ministères et célébration de l'eucharistie*, 198–204; M. Bevenot, 'Tertullian's Thoughts about the Christian Priesthood', in *Corona Gratiarum* I, Bruges 1975.

40. See Ignatius, Smyrn. 8.1f.; M. Jourgon, 'La présidence de l'eucharistie chez Ignace d'Antioche', *Lumière et Vie* 16, 1967, 26–32; R. Padberg, 'Das Amtsverständnis der Ignatiusbriefe', *Theologie und Glaube* 62, 1972, 47–54; H. Legrand, 'La présidence de l'eucharistie selon la tradition ancienne', *Spiritus* 18, 1977, 409–31. See ch. I, n. 16.

41. Cyprian, *Epist.* 45.

42. Cyprian, *Litt.* 69.9.3; 72.2.1; *De unitate Ecclesiae* 17.

43. This is a tradition which applied until the Middle Ages in both East and West. See e.g. Jerome, *Epist.* 15.2; Innocent I, *Epist.* 24.3; Leo, *Epist.* 80.2; Pelagius I, *Epist.* 24.14; Aphraates, *Dem. 12 de Paschate* 9; *Decr. Gratiani* II, c. 1, q. 1, chs. 73 and 78; Peter Lombard, *Sent.* IV, d. 13.

44. To be found in *Vita Zephyrini* 2 (ed. L. Duchesne I, 139f.).

45. See D. Droste, *Celebrare in der Römischen Liturgiesprache*, Munich 1963, above all 73–80; R. Schultze, *Die Messe als Opfer der Kirche*, Münster 1959; R. Raes, 'La concélébration eucharistique dans les rites orientaux', *La Maison-Dieu* 35, 1953, 24–47; R. Berger, *Die Wendung* offerre pro *in der römischen Liturgie*, Munster 1965; Y. Congar, 'L'Ecclesia ou communauté chrétienne sujet intégral de l'action liturgique', in *La liturgie d'apres Vatican II*, Paris 1967, 241–82; E. Dekkers, 'La concélébration, tradition ou nouveauté?', in *Mélanges Liturgiques*, Louvain 1972, 99–120; B. Botte, 'Notè historique sur la concélébration dans l'Eglise ancienne', *La Maison-Dieu* 35, 1953, 9–23.

46. For an apparent exception see the Gelasianum, Droste, op. cit., 80.

47. Even at the end of the eleventh century, Guerricus of Igny writes: 'The priest does not consecrate by himself, he does not offer by himself, but the whole assembly of believers *consecrates and offers* along with him' (*Sermo* 5; PL 185.57).

48. See above all E. Dekkers, op. cit., n. 45, 110–12; R. Berger, op. cit., 246; R. Schultze, op. cit., 188.

49. I Clement 44.4–6. See M. Jourgon, 'Remarques sur le vocabulaire sacerdotal de la Prima Clementis', in *Epektasis* (In honour of Cardinal J. Daniélou), Paris 1972, 109; J. Blond, in *L'eucharistie des premiers chrétiens*, Paris 1948, 38f. ·

50. See Ch. II, n. 40.

51. Tertullian, *De Exhort. Cast.* 7.3; cf. *De Praescriptione* 41, 5–8. G. Otranto, '*Nonne et laici sacerdotes sumus?*' (*Exhort. Cast.* 7.3), in *Vetera Christianorum* 8, 1971, 27–47.

52. See G. Otranto, 'Il sacerdozio commune del fideli nei reflessi della I Petr. 3,9', in *Vetera Christianorum* 7, 1970, 225–46. See J. Delorme, 'Sacerdoce du Christ et ministère (à propos de Jean 17)', *RSR* 62, 1974, 199–219; J. H. Elliott, *The Elect and the Holy. An Exegetical Examination of I Peter 2.4–10*, Leiden 1966 (the term 'priestly people of God' does not have any cultic significance; this expression indicates the election of the Christian community).

53. Augustine, *Litt.* 3.8: CSEL 34, 655.

54. See Ch. II n. 51.

55. We may well ask how far the Western repetitions of canon 6 of Chalcedon are simply the result of the work of intellectuals – canonical anthologies – without any explicit reflection of the church's practice which had developed in the feudal period and without much influence on it. The new practice which had developed from below prepared for the later new canonical regulations. This fact is also instructive!

56. *Concilium Lateranense* III (1179), ch. 5: Mansi, *Conc.* XXII, 220. Instead of *titulus ecclesiae* or ecclesial appointment, we now have, in pure feudal terms, '*sine certo titulo de quo necessaria vitae percipiat*' (loc. cit.); the *stipendia convenientia* must be assured. How necessary this regulation was, given the chaos in previous centuries, is evident from R. Foreville, *Latran I, II, III et Latran IV* (Histoire des conciles oecumeniques 6), Paris 1965, who also publishes the whole of the text of Lateran III, 210–13, and not one decree from it, like Denzinger, which puts the whole of the reforming significance of this council out of joint and disguises the fact that the council in no way sought to make a break with the patristic tradition. See also V. Fuchs, *Der ordinationstitel* (Chapter II, n. 1). In fact a Roman synod had already allowed absolute ordinations in 1099 (Mansi XX, 806, and 970), as a dispensation.

57. Clearly an attempt to update the old tradition in the difficult financial context of feudalism (Innocent III, *Ep. ad Zamorensem episcopum*: ed. Friedberg, *Corpus Iuris Canonici* II, 469). Urban II (1088) already recognized consecrations *sine titulo Ecclesiae*: Mansi XX, 970; however, this was probably seen as a consequence of the increase in papal power

which could 'dispense' even with church laws. See A. Schebler, *Die Reordinationen*, 277; see also the literature quoted in Ch. IV, n. 6.

58. See below.

59. Thus here the validity has become independent of the vocation and sending by a local community (Lateran IV, a. 1215, c. 1: Denzinger-Schönmetzer 802).

60. In fact for the first time in official church documents in 1201 there is mention of a 'character of baptism' (Pope Innocent III: Denzinger-Schönmetzer 781), and in 1231 of a priestly character (Pope Gregory IX, Denzinger-Schönmetzer 825). I very much doubt whether this had the sacral-mystical significance in the Middle Ages which was assigned to it in subsequent centuries. B. McSweeney ('The Priesthood in Sociological Theory', *Social Compass* 21, 1974, 5–25) may advance relevant sociological insights, but his historical appreciations seem to me to be very crude.

61. See E. Schillebeeckx, *Sacramentele heilseconomie*, Bilthoven/Antwerp 1952, 185–98, and s.v. 'Merkteken', in *Theologische Woordenboek* 2, 3231–237.

62. A. Poeschl, 'Die Entstehung des geistlichen Benefiziums', *Archiv für katholische Kirchenrecht* 106, 1926, 3–121, and 363–471; A. Werminghoff, in *Monumenta Historica Germanicae, Legum Sectio III, Concilia II, Concilia Aevi Karolini* I, Hanover/Leipzig 1908; see also F. Oediger, *Über die Bildung der Geistlichen im Späten Mittelalter*, Leiden 1953.

63. *Speculum doctrinale* VIII, 34. See G. de Lagarde, *La naissance de l'esprit laïque au declin du Moyen-Age, I: Bilan du XIIIᵉ siècle*, Paris-Louvain 1956; the emergence of the juridical idea of *plenitudo potestatis*.

64. The emphasis on the clergy is already evident in the Carolingian period. The earlier ecclesial terminology, *conficere, consecrare, immolare* – actions of which earlier the whole of the community was the active subject – is gradually limited to the clergy's own actions. The earlier *tota aetas concelebrat* (*Vita Zephyrini*, 2: ed. L. Duchesne I, 139f.) now becomes: what the priest does is simply done *in voto* by the whole of the believing people of God (*inter alia* Innocent III, *De sacro altaris mysterio* III, 6: PL 217, 845).

65. See R. J. Cox, *A Study of the Juridic Status of Laymen in the Writings of the Mediaeval Canonist*, Washington 1959; L. Hödl, *Die Geschichte der scholastischen Literatur und der Theologie der Schlüsselgewalt*, Münster 1960; W. Plöchl, *Geschichte des Kirchenrechts*, Vienna ²1960, I, 224ff.; K. J. Becker, *Wesen und Vollmachten des Priestertums nach dem Lehramt*, Quaestiones disputatae 47, Freiburg 1970, 113–21; M. van de Kerckhove, 'La notion de juridiction dans la doctrine des Décrétistes et des premiers Décrétalistes, de Gratien (1140) à Bernard de Bottone', *Etudes Franciscans* 49, 1937, 42–55; P. Krämer, *Dienst und Vollmacht in der Kirche: Eine rechtstheologische Untersuchung zur Sacra Potestas-Lehre des II. Vatikanischen Konzils*, Trier 1973; Y. Congar, *Sainte Eglise*, Paris 1963, 203–38; id., 'R. Sohm nous interroge encore', *RSPT* 57, 1973, 263–94; J. Ratzinger, 'Opfer, Sakramentum und Priestertum in der Entwicklung

der Kirche', *Catholica* 26, 1972, 108–25, and id., *Das neue Volk Gottes*, Düsseldorf ²1970, 75–245.

66. For the consequences and above all the development of the private mass see *inter alia* O. Nussbaum, *Kloster, Priestermönch und Privatmesse*, Bonn 1961; A. Haussling, *Mönchskonvent und Eucharistiefeier*, Münster 1973; id., 'Ursprünge der Privatmesse', *Stimme der Zeit* 90, 1964–65, 21ff.

67. I am in no way denying the value of a private mass as deep personal prayer, much less its formative value for the priest who celebrates it; I am simply saying that in terms of the priestly ministry and the church, at the least it is very peripheral. A sacrament is the celebration of a local community (of whom a large number will be present), not of a community 'envisaged as being there'.

68. For the emergence of the mediaeval principle of dispensation, above all from Hinkmar of Reims on, see E. Plazinski, *Mit Krummstab und Mitra*, Buisdorf 1970; V. Fuchs, *Die Ordinationstitel* (see Ch. II n. 1); M. A. Stiegler, *Dispensation*, Mainz 1908, with further literature in Ch. IV n. 6.

69. H. de Lubac, *Corpus mysticum: L'eucharistie et l'Eglise au moyenage*, Paris ²1949, esp. ch. 5, also Y. Congar, *L'Eglise de saint Augustin à l'époque moderne*, Histoire des dogmes III/3, Paris 1970, 167–73 (= Handbuch der Dogmengeschichte III-3c, Freiburg 1971, 105–8).

70. *In IV Sent.*, d. 24, q. 2, a. 2, ad 2. Like the whole of scholasticism Thomas also says: *sacramentum ordinis ordinatur ad eucharistiae consecrationem* (*Summa Theologiae* III, 2.65 a. 3). Although I have already said that above all in the first four centuries the ministry was primarily seen in relation to the building up of the community and in that to the eucharistic nucleus of any Christian community, we have to concede that from the end of the fourth century, with the origin of the canonical law of abstention, which was seen in terms of abstention before the eucharist (see Ch. IV below), as time went on at least the emphasis came to be placed on the altar service of the priest which also involved this far-reaching canonical legislation. See J. P-Audet, *Mariage et Celibat dans le service pastoral de l'Eglise*, Paris 1967, pp. 10f., 124–35.

71. See above all J. P. Massaut, *Josse Clichtove, l'humanisme et la reforme du clergé*, two vols, Paris 1969; id., 'Vers la Réforme catholique. Le célibat dans l'idéal sacerdotal de Josse Clichtove', in *Sacerdoce et célibat* (In Memory of J. Coppens), Gembloux-Louvain 1971, 459–506; id., 'Théologie Universitaire et Requêtes Spirituelles (un texte inedit de Josse Clichtove)', in *La Controverse Religieuse (XVIᵉ-XIXᵉ siecles)*, Actes du Premier Colloque Jean Boisset, Montpellier 1980, 7–18. (I am grateful to J. P. Massaut, who has drawn my attention to these works since my contribution to *Minister? Pastor? Prophet?*, SCM Press and Crossroad Publishing Co. 1980). Also G. Chantraine, 'J. Clichtove: témoin théologique de l'humanisme parisien. Scolastique et célibat au XVIᵉ siecle', *RHE* 66, 1971, 507–28.

72. *'Non est autem essentialiter annexum debitum continentiae ordini sacro, sed ex statuto Ecclesiae: unde videtur quod per Ecclesiam potest dispensari*

in voto continentiae solemnizato per susceptionem sacri ordinis' (*Summa Theologiae* II–II, 2.66, a.11).

73. For the Tridentine doctrine of the ministry, see *inter alia*: E. Boularand, 'Le sacerdoce de la loi nouvelle d'après le decret du Concile de Trente sur le sacrement de l'ordre', *BLE* 56, 1955, 193–228; K. Becker, *Der priesterliche Dienst*, Vol. 2, *Wesen und Vollmachten des Priestertums nach dem Lehramt* (Questiones Disputatae 47), Freiburg 1970; A. Duval, 'Les données dogmatiques du Concile de Trente sur le sacerdoce', *Bulletin du Comité des Etudes* 38–39, vols 3–4, Paris 1962, 448–72; G. Fahrnberger, *Bischofsamt und Priestertum in den Diskussionen des Konzils von Trient. Eine Rechtstheologische Untersuchung*, Wiener Beiträge zur Theologie 30, Vienna 1970: A. Ganoczy, ' "Splendours and Miseries" of the Tridentine Doctrine of Ministries', *Concilium* 8, 1972, no. 10, 75–86; H. Jedin, *Geschichte des Konzils von Trient*, four vols, Freiburg 1949–75; 'Das Leitbild des Priesters nach dem Tridentinum und dem Vaticanum II', *Theologie und Glaube* 60, 1970, 102–24, and *Vaticanum II und Tridentinum. Tradition und Fortschritt in der Kirchengeschichte*, Cologne-Opladen 1963; P. Fransen, 'Le Concile de Trente et le sacerdoce', in *Le Prêtre, Foi et Contestation*, Gembloux-Paris 1969; L. Lescrauwaet, 'Trente en Vaticanum II over het dienstpriesterschap', *Ons Geestelijk Leven* 47, 1970, 194–205; J. Pegon, 'Episcopat et hiérarchie au Concile de Trente', *Nouvelle Revue Théologique* 82, 1960, 580–8; H. Reumkens, *Priesterschap en presbyteraat volgens het concile van Trente* (Doctoral dissertation), Tilburg 1974; E. Schillebeeckx, *Christus' tegenwoordigheid in de eucharistie*, Bilthoven 1967; *Handbuch der Dogmengeschichte*, Freiburg 1969, Vol. VI–5.

74. See A. Duval, 'L'Ordre au concile de Trente', in *Le Prêtre. Foi et Contestation*, 277ff.

75. The bishop of Avignon, see *Concilium Tridentinum* (ed. Societas Goeresiana), Freiburg 1901–61, Vol. 9, 83.

76. See Denziger-Schönmetzer, 1771–8: *de capita*; 1763–70. Above all: *'Hoc autem (sacramentum ordinis) ab eodem Domino Salvatore nostro institutum esse, atque apostolis eorumque successoribus in sacerdotio potestatem traditam consecrandi, offerendi et ministrandi corpus et sanguinem eius, necnon et peccata dimittendi . . .'* (Denziger-Schönmetzer 1764). And: *'Si quis dixerit, in Ecclesia non esse hierarchiam, divina ordinatione institutam quae constat ex episcopis, presbuteris et ministris, a.s.'* (Denziger-Schönmetzer 1776; to be compared with Vatican II, *Lumen Gentium*, no. 28).

77. Speeches by the bishops of Modena and Ugento, *Conc. Trident.*, 9.81 and 30.

78. See e.g. P. Fransen, 'L'autorité des conciles', in *Problèmes de l'autorité*, Paris 1962, 59–100, and *Le concile de Trente*, Ch. II n.73.

79. See A. Rohrbasser (ed.) *Sacerdotis imago. Päpstliche Dokumente über das Prietertum von Pius X bis Johannes XXIII*, Fribourg 1962.

Chapter III Continuity and Divergence between the First and Second Christian Millennia

1. Vatican II often still locates the *repraesentatio Christi* by the priest in the minister as a person, and not formally in the act of his exercising the ministry: 'through the *ordo* the priests are consecrated to God in a new way '(*Presbyterorum ordinis*, no. 12). See P. J. Cordes, *Sendung zum Dienst: Exegetisch-historische und systematische Studien zum Konzilsdebat 'Vom Dienst und Leben der Priester'*, Frankfurt 1972, 202. From the abundance of post-Vatican literature on the question see above all A. Acerbi, *Due ecclesiologie: Ecclesiologia giuridica ed ecclesiologia di communione nella 'Lumen Gentium'*, Bologna 1975; H. L. Legrand, 'Nature de l'Eglise particulière et rôle de l'évêque dans l'Eglise', in *La charge pastorale des évêques*, Unam Sanctam 74, Paris 1969, 115ff.; P. Krämer, *Dienst und Vollmacht in der Kirche* (see Ch. II, n. 65); K. J. Becker, *Wesen und Vollmachten* (ch. II, n. 65); Y. Congar, Preface to B. D. Marliangeas, *Clés pour une théologie du ministère: In persona Christi, In persona Ecclesiae*, Paris 1978, 5–14. Even the insertion of the concept of *communio hierarchica* (*Lumen Gentium* nos. 21 and 22, and above all Nota praevia) alongside the concept of the church as *communio* cannot bring any real harmony between *sacramentum* and *ius*; see a precise study of this lame concept in Cordes, *Sendung zum Dienst*, 291–301. The reasons for these unevennesses become clear from the *Expensio modorum* in the decree *Presbyterorum Ordinis*.

2. *Acta Apostolicae Sedis* 69, 1977, 98–116, esp. 109–113.

3. *Inter alia*, L. A. Hoedemaker, 'De moeizame gang naar de oekumena: multilaterale consensusvorming tussen kerken', *TvT* 18, 1978, 3–25; J. Lescrauwaet, 'Consensus over ambt en wijding', *TvT* 15, 1975, 269–90; *Amt und Ordination in ökumenischen Licht*, Quaestiones disputatae 50, Freiburg 1973; K. Rahner, *Vorfragen zu einem ökumenischen Amtsverständis*, Quaestiones disputatae 65, Freiburg 1974; *Dienst und Amt*, Regensburg 1973; *Ordination heute*, Kassel 1972; A. Houtepen, 'Eigentijds leergezag: Een oecumenische discussie', *TvT* 18, 1978, 26–48; *Intercommunion and Church Membership*, Tenth Downside Symposium, edited by J. Kent and R. Murray, London/Denville NJ 1973; E. Persson, 'The Two Ways: Some reflections on the Problem of the Ministry within Faith and Order 1927–1964', *Ecumenical Review* 17, 1965, 232–40; H. Schütte, *Amt, Ordination und Sukzession im Verständnis evangelischer und katholischer Exegeten und Dogmatiker der Gegenwart in Dokumenten ökumenischer Gespräche*, Düsseldorf 1974: *Modern Ecumenical Documents on the Ministry*, London 1975; 'Intercommunie en ambt', in *Archief van de Kerken* 33, 1978, 1–18; 'Doop, eucharistie en ambt,' op. cit., 21–31; 'Geloof en kerkorde', op. cit., 31–48.

4. Thomas, *In IV Sent.* d. 24, q. 3, a. 3, ad. 3.

5. *Lumen Gentium*, no. 21.

6. I Clement 40.4f. (see J. Fischer, *Die Apostolische Väter*, Darmstadt 1966, 17).

7. See *Traditio Hippolyti* 3 (Botte, ed. 1963, 9f.), where it is said that the bishop must co-ordinate the *kleroi*, i.e. the various ministerial tasks.

8. As to method, it should be noted in passing that the decree *Presbyterorum ordinis* must be interpreted in the light of the dogmatic constitution *Lumen Gentium*, and not vice versa.

9. *'Ordo dupliciter dicitur. Uno modo dicitur ordo ipsa relatio ordinatorum, ut* praelatio *et* subiectio; *et* haec non dicitur nec est sacramentum; *alio modo dicitur ordo ordinata potestas, secundum quam ipsum subiectum potens habet ordinari dupliciter, scilicet ad opus vel ad ministerium, et habet ordinari ad alterum; hanc autem potestatem dicimus ordinis sacramentum'* (Bonaventura, *In IV Sent.*, d. 24, p. 1, a. 2, q. 2); this is given a somewhat different slant in Thomas: *'Dicendum quod subiectio servitutis repugnat libertati; quae servitus est cum aliquis dominatur ad sui utilitatem subiectis utens. Talis autem subiectio non requiritur in ordine, per quem qui praesunt, salutem subditorum quaerere debent, non propter utilitatem'* (Thomas, *In IV Sent.*, d. 24, q. 1, a. 1, qla 1, ad I).

10. Literature in Ch. II, n. 1.

11. See B. D. Dupuy, 'Theologie der kirchlichen Ämter', in *Das Heilsgeschehen in der Gemeinde*, Mysterium Salutis IV/2, Einsiedeln 1973, 488–525 (the quotation comes from p. 495).

12. J. D. Zizioulas, 'Ordination et communion', *Istina* 16, 1971, 5–12, and in *Amt und Ordination in ökumenischen Sicht*, Quaestiones Disputatae 50, Freiburg 1973, 72–113.

13. Cf. Dupuy, op. cit. (n. 56), 514; Schillebeeckx, 'Priesterschap', 3959–4003.

14. H. M. Legrand, 'The "Indelible" Character and the Theology of Ministry', *Concilium* 8, 1972, no. 4, 54–62; P. Fransen, 'Wording en strekking van de canon over het merkteken te Trente', *Bijdr* 32, 1971, 2–34; F. Flamand, 'Réflexions pour une intelligence renouvelée du caractère sacerdotal', in *Le Prêtre, hier, aujourd'hui, demain*, Paris/Montreal 1970; N. Haring, 'St Augustine's Use of the Word Character', *Mediaeval Studies* 14, 1952, 79–97; id., 'Character, *Signum* und *Signaculum*: Die Entwicklung bis nach der karolingischen Renaissance', *Schol* 30, 1955, 481–512 and 31, 1956, 41–69, 182–212; J. Moingt, 'Caractère et ministère sacerdotal', *RSR* 56, 1968, 563–9; P. van Beneden, 'Het sacramenteel merkteken van de ambtsverlening', *TvT* 8, 1968, 140–54; J. Lecuyer, *L'ordre* (Somme Théol), Paris 1968; Schillebeeckx, *De sacramentele heilseconomie*, 501–36; id., 'Merkteken', 3231–7; E. Dassman, *Charakter indelebilis: Anpassung oder Verlegenheit?*, Cologne 1973.

15. Denziger-Schönmetzer, 781 and 825.

16. Schillebeeckx, *De sacramentele heilseconomie*, 501–4. The *Decretum pro Armenis* (Denziger-Schönmetzer, 1310–28) does not have the status of an ecumenical council.

17. This ontologizing in modern times, above all in the spirituality of the priesthood, emerges *inter alia* from the theory of J. Galot, who makes the character the foundation of priestly celibacy ('Sacerdoce et celibat', *NRT* 86, 1964, 119–24).

18. See *De vita S. Gregorii Thaumaturgi*, PG 46, 909. Later, small

non-urban communities got not an episcopal but a presbyteral leader (Schillebeeckx, 'Priesterschap', 3975–80, 3983–92). Here the old term presbyter in fact shifts towards that of priest. This historical shift gave rise in the Middle Ages to the discussion whether priest and bishop were not equal in respect to the power of ordination. A very pertinent question within the new conception of the ministry!

19. Present-day rejection in the Roman Catholic church of both the priesthood of a married man and the ordained ministry of women is discussed on pp. 85–99, 105–126.

20. See J. Ludwig, *Tu es Petrus*, Münster 1952; O. Cullmann, *Peter*, London and Philadelphia ²1962; B. Botte, 'Le Saint Pierre d'Oscar Cullmann', *Irenikon* 26, 1953, 140–5; L. Hertling, 'Communio und Primat: Kirche und Papsttum in der christlichen Antike', *Una Sancta* 17, 1962, 91–5; W. de Vries, *Rome und die Patriarchate des Ostens*, Freiburg/Munich 1963; 'La primauté dans l'Eglise dans la perspective de l'histoire du salut', *Istina* 8, 1961–62, 335–57; *Petrus und Papst*, ed. A. Brandenburg and H. J. Urban, Münster 1977; *Das Petrusamt in der gegenwärtigen theologischen Diskussion*, ed. H. J. Mund, Paderborn 1976; *Zum Wesen und Auftrag des Petrusamtes*, ed. J. Ratzinger, Düsseldorf 1978; K. H. Ohlig, *Braucht die Kirche einen Papst?* Mainz/Düsseldorf 1973.

21. *Inter alia, Lumen Gentium*, nos. 23, 25; *Christus Dominus*, no. 11; etc. (ET in *The Documents of Vatican II*, ed. Walter M. Abbott, Geoffrey Chapman 1965). See also H. Marot, 'Note sur l'expression "*episcopus catholicae Ecclesiae*" ', *Irenikon* 37, 1964, 221–6.

22. Against Karl Rahner, above all in *Das Amt der Einheit*, Stuttgart 1964, see rightly H. M. Legrand, 'Nature de l'Eglise' (Ch. III, n. 1), 105–21, and id, 'The Revaluation of Local Churches. Some Theological Implications', *Concilium* 8, 1972, no. 1, 53–64; L. Ott, *Le sacrement de l'Ordre*, Paris 1971, esp. 42–4. I am sceptical about what seems to me to be the anachronistic conclusion which is often drawn from this, that even now the Pope, as bishop of the local church of Rome, should be chosen by the Christians and clergy of Rome – the one-sided basic position of the number of *Concilium* on the Papacy. See the good studies in *Le concile et les conciles*, ed. B. Botte et al., Paris 1960.

Chapter IV   Tension between Actual Church Order and
Alternative Practices in the Ministry

1. *Lumen Gentium*, no. 28.
2. Mansi II, 469.
3. J. Beyer, 'Nature et position du sacerdoce', *NRT* 76, 1954, 356–73, 469–80; Y. Congar, *Sainte Eglise*, Unam Sanctam 41, Paris 1963, 275–302; W. Kasper, 'Zur Frage der Anerkennung der Ämter in der katholischen Kirche', *TQ* 151, 1971, 97–102. Cf. F. J. Beeck, 'Extraordinary Ministries of All or Most of the Sacraments', *JES* 3, 1966, 57–112.
4. See Y. Congar, '*Supplet Ecclesia*: propos en vue d'une théologie de l'économie dans la tradition latine', *Irenikon* 45, 1972, 155–207; H.

Herrmann, *Ecclesia supplet. Das Rechtinstitut der kirchlichen Suppletion nach can. 209. C.I.C.*, Amsterdam 1968.

5. See F. Gillmann, *Die Notwendigkeit der Intention auf Seiten des Spenders und des Empfangers der Sakramente nach Anschauung der Frühscholastik*, Mains 1916; A. Landgraf, *Dogmengeschichte der Frühscholastik*, Regensburg 1955, III–1, 109–68; IV–2, 223–43.

6. F. Planzinski, *Mit Krummstab und Mitra*, Buisdorf 1970; M. A. Stiegler, *Dispensation. Dispensationswesen und Dispensationsrecht in Kirchenrecht geschichtlich dargestellt*, Mainz 1908; A. Schebler, *Die Reordinationen in der altkatholischen Kirche unter besonderer Berücksichtigung der Anschauungen Rudolphs Sohms*, Bonn 1936; L. Saltet, *Les réordinations*, Paris 1907; L. Buisson, *Potestas et Caritas. Die päpstliche Gewalt im Spätmittelalter*, Cologne-Graz 1958. The Western principle of dispensation differs on a number of points from the common Eastern *oikonomia* principle. See M. Widmann, *Der Begriff Oikonomia im Werk des Irenaeus und seine Vorgeschichte*, Tübingen 1956; F. J. Thompson, 'Economy', *JTS* NS 16, 1965, 368–420; Mgr J. Kotsonis, *Problèmes de l'économie ecclésiastique*, Gembloux 1971; Mgr P. l'Huillier, 'Economie et Théologie Sacramentaire', *Istina* 17, 1972, 17–20; K. McDonnell, 'Ways of Validating Ministry', *JES* 7, 1970, 209–65; K. Duchatelez, 'De geldigheid van de wijdingen in het licht der "economie" ', *TvT* 8, 1968, 377–401; P. Dumont, 'Economie ecclésiastique et réitération des sacraments', *Irenikon* 14, 1937, 228–47 and 339–62; Y. Congar, 'Quelques Problèmes touchant les ministères', *NRT* 93, 1971, 785–800.

7. Y. Congar, 'Reception as an Ecclesiological Reality', *Concilium* 8, 1972, no. 7, 43f.; there is a more extended version in 'La "reception" comme réalité ecclésiologique', *RSPT* 56, 1972, 369–403; see also Congar, '*Quod omnes tangit ab omnibus tractari et approbari debet*', *Revue historique de Droit français et étranger* 36, 1958, 210–59; A. Grillmeier, 'Konzil und Reception', in *Mit ihm und in ihm. Christologische Farschungen und Perspektiven*, Freiburg 1975, 303–34.

8. Denzinger-Schönmetzer no. 1728, see E. Schillebeeckx, *De sacramentele heilseconomie*, Antwerp-Bilthoven 1952, 416–51.

9. Mansi, 20, 970. See A. Schebler, *Die Reordinationen* (n. 6), 277f.

10. For new literature (after my book *Het ambtscelibaat in de branding*, Bilthoven 1965, which provides historical correction at some points), see especially G. Denzler, *Das Papsttum und der Amtszölibat*, two vols, Stuttgart 1973, 1976; H.-J. Vogels, *Pflicht-zölibat. Eine kritische Untersuchung*, Munich 1978; R. Gryson, *Les origines du célibat ecclésiastique du premier au septième siecle*, Gembloux 1970, and 'Dix ans de recherches sur les origines du célibat ecclésiastique', *Revue Théologique de Louvain* 11, 1980, 157–85; N. Grévy-Pons, *Célibat et nature. Une controverse mediévale*, Paris 1975. See also the earlier study R. Bultot, *La doctrine du mépris du monde*, Louvain-Paris 1963ff. See also the literature in nn. 11, 14, 15, 20, 21 below.

11. See R. Kottje, 'Das Aufkommen der täglichen Eucharistiefeier in der Westkirche und die Zölibatsforderung', in *ZKG* 81, 1971, 218–88; L. Hodl, 'Die *lex continentiae*', in *ZKT* 83, 1961, 325–43.

12. Civil: *Codex Theodosii* XVI, 2, 44; canonical: *Canones Apostolorum* 5.

13. *Acta Apostolicae Sedis* 66, 1954, 169f.

14. E. Fehrle, *Die Kultische Keuschheit im Altertum* (Religionsgeschichtliche Versuche und Vorarbeiten 6), Giessen 1910. Of course this author neglects Eastern influences on this Hellenism: see H. Jeanmaire, 'Sexualité et mysticisme dans les anciennes sociétés helléniques', in *Mystique et Continence*, Etudes Carmélitaines, Paris-Bruges 1952, 51–60.

15. *Inter alia* (in addition to the standard literature on the Stoa and Neo-Platonism), see a good short summary by G. Delling, s.v. 'Geschlechtsverkehr', in *RAC* 10, 1977, 812–29.

16. See A. Vööbus, *Celibacy. A Requirement for Admission to Baptism in the Syriac Church*, Stockholm 1951; K. Muller, *Die Forderung der Ehelosigkeit für alle Getauften in der alten Kirche*, Tübingen 1927; E. Schillebeeckx, *Het Huwelijk. Aardse werkelijkheid en heilsmysterie*, Vol. 1, Bilthoven 1963, 171.

17. Jerome, *Ad Jovinianum* I, 20: PL 23, 238; see also I, 34; PL 23, 256–8. See the same reasoning throughout the patristic literature, *inter alia* II Clement 14.3–5; 12.2, 5, above all the book by the Pythagorean Sextus, which was a favourite among Christians (Origen, *Contra Celsum* 8, 30), in which it is said that 'praying' and 'sexual intercourse' cannot go together and are by nature contradictory so that 'castration' is commended as the only way. This left a great impression on many Christians of the time. Origen himself adopted this means literally. See also in the same spirit: Ambrose, *De officiis ministrorum* I, 50: PL 16, 98; Innocent I, *Epistula ad Victricium*, ch. 10: PL 56, 523; *Epistula ad Exsuperium* c. 1: PL 56, 501; Pope Siricius, *Epist. ad Episcopos Africae*: PL 56, 728; Augustine, *De coniugiis adulterimis*, II, 21; PL 40, 486. Furthermore, in patristic literature we find the universal human complaints about married life in a frivolous sense, *inter alia* Ambrose, *De Virginibus* I, n. 6, 25f.: PL 16, 195f.; Basil, *Epist.* II, 2: PG 32, 224f.; Jerome, *Adversus Helvidium* 22: PL 23, 206; Ambrose, *De viduis*, ch. 13 n. 81: PL 16, 259; Gregory of Nyssa, *De virginitate* 3: PG 46, 325–36; Tertullian, *Ad uxorem* I, 5: PL 1, 1282f. We also find this satyrical type of literature about marriage in the pagan writings of the time; see P. de Labriolle, *Les satires de Juvénal. Etude et analyse*, Paris n.d., 129–7. However, these universal human satires on married life, to be taken with a pinch of salt, served in patristic literature the 'excessive motivation' of Christian abstinence, which at this time was clearly influenced by Hellenistic encratism or hostility to all sexuality.

18. Denzinger did not take this canon, which had such far-reaching influence on the Latin church, into his collection of 'important' church documents. See *Conciliorum Oecumenicorum Decreta* (ed. G. Alberigo et al.), Freiburg 1962, 174f. Furthermore in its canon 7 this Council compels priests who are already legitimately married to send away their wives. This is completely incomprehensible in terms of the canon law

of the church and in the light of the Bible. There is no thought as to the fate of the wife.

19. A precise study of this history can be found in M. Dortel-Claudot, 'Le prêtre et le mariage: évolution de la législation canonique des origines au XIIᵉ siecle', in *L'Année Canonique* 17, 1973, 319–44; also E. J. Jonkers, 'De strijd om het celibaat van geestlijken van de vierde tot de tiende eeuw in het Westen volgens de Conciles', *Nederlands Archief voor Kerkgeschiedenis* 57, 1976–77, 129–44.

20. See the careful study, already cited in a previous chapter, by P. H. Lafontaine, *Les conditions positives de l'accession aux ordres dans la première législation ecclésiastique (300–492)*, Ottawa 1963, above all 71ff.

21. For the confiscation of goods in this connection see, *inter alia*, Synod of Pavia (beginning of the eleventh century), c. 3: Mansi, *Conc* 19, 353; Synod of Rome (1059): Mansi, *Conc* 18, 897f.; Synod of Rome (1074): Mansi, *Conc* 20, 424; Synod of Amalfi (1089): Mansi, *Conc* 20, 724; the Second Lateran Council: Mansi, *Conc* 21, 526ff.

22. *Concilium Tridentinum* (Societas Goerresiana), Vol. 9, 640, 660–9.

23. 'Law of celibacy' is not my terminology but that of the official church documents, see *inter alia* the *Motu Proprio* of Paul VI, *Sacrum diaconatus Ordinem* of 18 June 1967, where there is clear mention of a *Lex caelibatus*, in *AAS* 59, 1967, 699, although as far as I remember this term is not to be found in the encyclical *Sacerdotalis Caelibatus* itself dating from the same year; see *AAS* 69, 1967, 657–97.

24. Pohier, *Au nom du Père*, Paris 1972, 171–223.

25. *Declaratio* of 15 October 1976, *AAS* 69, 1977, 98–116.

26. See 'La question du ministère en Afrique', *Spiritus* 18, 1977, 358.

27. Op. cit., 359. See the pithy commentary on this by C. Duquoc, 'Théologie de l'Eglise et crise du ministère', *Études* 350, 1979, 101–14, and the reaction by the auxiliary bishop of Paris, Mgr E. Marcus, 'L'appel au presbytérat', *Études* 350, 1979, no. 3, 415–23.

Chapter VI　Some Perspectives on the Future: Contextual Experience of Ministry within a Living Community

1. This synod is the third synod since Vatican II. Officially it is called the 'second synod', because the previous one was an 'extraordinary synod'.

2. *Le ministère sacerdotal* (Rapport de la Commission Internationale de Théologie), Editions du Cerf, Paris 1972. The six points are to be found there on pp. 125f.

3. 'Itinera fidelitatis sunt semper et necessario itinera creativitatis . . . Duae theologiae de proposita quaestione nobis offerentur: una quae initium sumit a conceptu sacerdotii, altera vero a conceptu ministerio sacerdotali . . . Bene prae oculis habeamus praesentem crisim sacerdotii solvi non posse ex theologia ex qua ex parte crisis orta est.'

4. Patriarch Maximus V. Hakim, successor to Maximus IV who was at the Second Vatican Council, clearly said in a speech at the synod: 'Pour nous, que nous le voulions ou non, de par l'extension géograph-

ique de la chrétienté, de par la fin de l'ère coloniale et le réveil des nationalismes légitimes, l'ère d'une Eglise identique et nivelée est définitivement passée. Nous sommes entrés dans l'ère des Eglises locales, dont la variété fait beauté et dont l'unité autour du Successeur de Pierre, n'est pas et ne peut plus être uniformité.'

5. '*Conamen facere ut systema quoddam intra aliud systema majus reformandi, sine mutatione systematis majoris, est utopicus*' (speech at the synod).

6. '*Tempus est ut dimittamus curam, nos ad mundum adaptandi – id quod termino vernaculo "aggiornamento" expressum est. Nunc est tempus ut, Christum sequentes, aliis duces simus*' (speech at the synod).

7. The final text has an insertion aimed at giving this aspect its full value: 'to the degree that this earthly process contributes to a better ordering of society' (see *Expensio modorum*, *Gaudium et Spes*, ch. 3, Part I, p. 236). The final text now runs: 'But the expectation of a new earth must not weaken the concern to develop this earth; rather, it must strengthen it. For it is here that there grows the body of the new family of mankind which is already to some degree in process of giving a foreshadowing of the final kingdom. Thus although developments on earth must be carefully distinguished from the kingdom of Christ, they are most profoundly involved in the kingdom of God in so far as they can contribute to a better ordering of human society' (*Gaudium et Spes* no. 39). Half an hour's *lectio divina* in the documents of Vatican II would have been most appropriate for the synod agenda.

8. Mgr A. Tortolo (Argentina): '*Unus Pater, invocata collegialitate, petivit ne clauderetur ianua. In nomine istius collegialitatis, liceat petere ne ianuam aperiatur.*'

9. '*Expedit quod caelibatus* libera optione *assumetur, habita ratione speciatim dignitatis personae humanae, "numquam enim homines tam acutum ut hodie sensum libertatis habuerunt*" (*Gaudium et Spes*, no. 4). *Hic est etiam consensus maioris partis cleri nostri, prout in investigationibus* (encuestas) *patet*' (Mgr Felipe Santiago Benitez, Paraguay).

10. There is no explicit mention of a 'principle of selection', but the speeches clearly come very near to that. It is formulated most clearly by Mgr P. J. Schmitt (Metz), speaking in the name of the synod of French bishops: 'En raison de l'union personelle du prêtre à Jésus-Christ et de sa consécration à la mission, *nous appellerons* au sacerdoce presbytéral *ceux qui*, par la grâce de Dieu, sont disposés a ce don total que constitue le célibat consacré dans "esprit évangélique". – En retour, nous nous sentons nous-mêmes engagés, avec tout le Peuple de Dieu, à leur offrir les conditions humaines, spirituelles et apostoliques d'une ministère qui corresponde au don de toute leur vie.' This is clearly an abandonment of the obligation that anyone who wants to become a priest should be celibate, but on the other hand the charisma of celibacy, already present and freely accepted, is regarded as a principle of selection for the choice of priests by the hierarchy. This spirit, then, at least makes a difference.

11. '*Moti sumus potius praesertim ex hac consideratione: ut (caelibatus)*

*retineat maximum valorem signi quem habet, opportet . . . etiam ut in omnium
communi aestimatione* videatur *esse talis, ablata omni obscuritate vel dubio
. . . Propter hanc rationem, membra Conferentiae Antiliarum sentiunt ordi-
nationem aliquorum hominum qui iam matrimonio sunt iuncti* medium esse
nostris diebus quasi necessarium *ad demonstrandum sacerdotes qui profiten-
tur caelibatum* hos facere animo verre libero et generoso, a nemine
coacto' (speech by Mgr S. Carter).

12. 'Ainsi que l'on s'abandonne pas au gré de chacun le charisme
du célibat. Il courait de trop grand risques' (Mgr B. Oguki-Atakpah,
from Togo). One of his arguments was: 'En tout cas, on ne m'a pas
encore montré ici à Rome la tombe de la femme de Pierre ou de Paul';
for him this was a providential sign for the celibacy of the priesthood.
I am aware of the 'humorous' value of such 'arguments', but this
nevertheless reveals their 'ideology'.

13. '*Ego certe non sum ex iis qui aliquo modo poetico vel nimis optimistico
consideret statum de facto quoad caelibatum sacerdotalem . . . Sed idem valet
etiam pro statu matrimonali . . .*' (speech).

14. 'On a l'impression que tout tourne autour de la sexualité, sous
pretexte que le mariage est un grand sacrément' (Mgr B. Oguki-Atakpah, from Togo).

15. Mgr J. Gran, living amongst married Lutheran pastors, gave this
evidence: 'In Scandinavia, where nearly everybody is Lutheran, the
clergy are normally married men. Divorce, desertion and the like rarely
occur. Most of the pastors appear to be truly spiritual persons, not
inferior to our Catholic priests. Moreover, they often possess a maturity
which must stem from their family responsibility. Their wives are very
much part of their vocation . . .' Although the bishop said this in a
speech in connection with the practical section, after him some other
bishops nevertheless painted the following picture of the disasters
which would occur if married men were to be ordained: divorce, birth
control, abortion, polygamy, priests' children who might behave badly
or even become hippies, nepotism, and so on.

16. Himself convinced that the celibacy of the priesthood should be
strictly maintained, Mgr J Diraviam, Archbishop of Madhurai (India)
nevertheless made the following remark, which is worth considering:
'The decision of the Synod will not be acceptable for lack of credibility
of the Synod, if the question has not been examined freely and without
prejudice as though the decision was already settled beforehand.'

17. With reference to the Pope's letter of 2 February 1970 to Cardinal
Villot, Cardinal Samore said: '*Haec Summi Pontificis verba manifeste eius
voluntatem patefaciunt, quae disceptationem circa caelibatum sic dictum op-
tionalem omnino* excludit . . . *Quapropter nec admittitur disceptatio qualis-
cumque in hac Synodo de readmissione ad ministerium sacerdotale illorum qui
ad statum laicalem reducti fuerint et matrimonium inierint.*'

18. '*Mihi, aperte dicam, pressio quae semper vehementior fit ab una parte
sacerdotum minime videtur signum temporis per quod Deus loquitur Ecclesiae*'
(speech).

19. The original text and a Dutch translation of this letter were published in *NRC Handelsblad*, Saturday 5 July 1980.

20. For 'integrated leadership' see J. Vollebergh, 'Religious Leadership', in *Minister? Pastor? Prophet?*, SCM Press and Crossroad Publishing Co. 1980, 41–56.

21. There does not seem any point in ending by giving a list of literature on the ministry; it is immense. The specialist group on dogmatic theology at the theological faculty of the Catholic University of Nijmegen (under the leadership of B. Willems) has issued a bibliography of the last ten years' publications on the ministry which includes more than four thousand titles. Those who are interested can have the time of their lives here!